J'aime P...

Inspirational Ideas for Introducing French to Young Children

Brilliant Publications

Ann May

We hope you and your pupils enjoy using the ideas in this book. Brilliant Publications publishes many other books for teaching modern foreign languages in primary schools. To find out more details on any of our titles, please log on to our website: www.brilliantpublications.co.uk.

100+ Fun Ideas for Practising Modern Foreign Languages
 in the Primary Classroom   978-1-903853-98-6

C'est Français!   978-1-903853-02-3
Chantez Plus Fort!   978-1-903853-37-5
French Pen Pals Made Easy   978-1-905780-10-5
Hexagonie 1   978-1-903853-92-4
J'aime Chanter!   978-1-905780-11-2
Jouons Tous Ensemble   978-1-903853-81-8

¡Es Español!   978-1-903853-64-1
Juguemos Todos Juntos   978-1-903853-95-5
¡Vamos a Cantar!   978-1-905780-13-6

Das ist Deutsch   978-1-905780-15-0
Wir Spielen Zusammen   978-1-903853-97-9

Giochiamo Tutti Insieme   978-1-903853-96-2

Flashcards (French, German, Italian and Spanish)
Actions (verbs)   978-1-905780-07-5
Everyday objects   978-1-905780-06-8
Food   978-1-905780-08-2
Opposites   978-1-905780-09-9

Published by Brilliant Publications
Unit 10
Sparrow Hall Farm
Edlesborough
Dunstable
Bedfordshire
LU6 2ES, UK

Sales and stock enquiries:
Tel: 01202 712910
Fax: 0845 1309300
E-mail: brilliant@bebc.co.uk
Website: www.brilliantpublications.co.uk

General information enquiries:
Tel: 01525 222292

The name Brilliant Publications and the logo are registered trademarks.

Written by Ann May
Illustrated by Gaynor Berry
Front cover designed by Gloss Solutions
Audio CD produced by Footstep Productions Ltd

Contents

Introduction

J'aime Parler! was conceived when I was trying to find material for Key Stage 1 children for an after-school French club I was running. I found that although there is a wealth of material for older children, there is not much that is really suitable for little ones, especially when you want to focus on listening and speaking skills, rather than reading and writing. This is why most of the activities in this book are aimed at oracy skills, so that the children become confident at speaking French, through repetition, role play, rhymes and songs. As young children are so receptive to acquiring different sounds through language, they will enjoy the activities and become competent in French quite quickly, without inhibitions.

I needed an activity to finish the lesson off with and decided that photocopiable colouring and drawing sheets would be a good activity for the children to focus on. The photocopiable sheets, which can be used during curriculum time or in clubs, complement some of the QCA schemes of work, but with Key Stage 1 in mind. All the sheets have been tried and tested and have been a source of delight to not only infants, but to younger juniors as well. The sheets are a welcome change after listening and speaking practice, and games and songs, and can be used as a colouring/drawing competition, for display work or can be taken home each week. During some of my half-hour-long lunchtime clubs, the children are delighted when I produce a sheet at the end of a topic or at the end of a half term.

It is my experience that many parents are very keen for their children to learn a foreign language at such a young age, and are very appreciative of the efforts that schools make for them in this subject. Also, having something to take home regularly encourages pupils to revise and practise, whilst communicating with, or even teaching, others at home. Many parents keep the sheets in a folder at home for children to revisit later. It is also very rewarding to see the children longing to show their parents the work when they are collected at the end of the day!

The CDs that accompany the course consist of stories that complement each lesson. The children will identify with Marvin the kitten, as he is a British kitten who finds himself in France, and does not understand the language. The children will gradually learn more and more French alongside Marvin who learns the language whilst having many varied adventures. The stories are designed to be used at the end of each lesson, to consolidate the language that has just been learnt. When the stories are played, the children should repeat the spoken French whenever there is a pause after a character speaks. This will promote confidence with listening and speaking skills. In addition, there are five traditional songs on the second CD.

How to use J'aime Parler!

There are 23 lesson plans in this book. Some lessons may require two or three sessions, depending on the time available. Most lessons, however, will only require one hour-long session. It is also a good idea to plan lessons that are totally devoted to revision every now and then. The lessons do not need to be taught in the order shown, although the vocabulary used gradually increases as you progress through the book.

If you have time left at the end of the academic year, this could be used for assessment, revision, or even rehearsals for an assembly or a show for the school or parents, using conversation, songs, rhymes and miming – the latter activity being a most rewarding event for all concerned! Assembly ideas are given on pages 87–88.

Each lesson plan contains:

Learning objective(s)
These are also listed on the Contents page, for quick reference.

Resources needed
Most of the additional resources suggested can easily be found in the classroom, although I have also suggested some optional resources (in particular French song books, see Song ideas below). The list of 'Useful resources' on page 104 gives addresses for some suppliers of French posters, song books, DVDs/videos and other materials.

Vocabulary
It is up to you to decide how much or how little vocabulary to introduce. I have chosen the vocabulary based on my experience of what works best for 5–7 year olds. I find it is best to teach lots of simple questions and answers. That way children can start having meaningful conversations in French quickly, and experience a real sense of accomplishment.

Recap
It is always a good idea to start the lesson with a recap on what they learned the lesson before. Some suggestions are given. However, if the lessons are not taught in the order shown, these ideas will need to be modified.

Ideas for introducing the vocabulary
With young children, it is always a good idea to start with a short discussion in English about the subject matter before teaching anything new in French, to avoid any confusion. I've suggested a variety of methods for introducing new vocabulary. Many of these techniques can be used, whatever the vocabulary being introduced.

Activities
Each lesson contains a variety of activities. You do not need to do all the activities and should use your professional judgement to decide which to include.

Song idea(s)

In addition I have suggested songs from two book and CD sets published by Brilliant Publications, *J'aime Chanter!* and *Chantez Plus Fort! J'aime Chanter!* is ideal for young children as the songs are set to familiar tunes, such as 'Ten green bottles' and 'Polly put the kettle on', so the children (and you!) can concentrate on learning the songs. The songs on *Chantez Plus Fort!* are set to original catchy tunes. As this book and CD set is aimed at Key Stage 2, you may find that some of the tunes are sung too fast on the CD for Key Stage 1 pupils. However, the tunes are easy to pick up, so the CD is not essential.

There are other song CDs available on the market (see Useful resources, page 104).

CD story

As mentioned in the introduction, one feature of *J'aime Parler!* is the stories on the CDs about Marvin, the British cat who finds himself in France. Encourage pupils to practise the French phrases in the pauses. You may wish to hold down the pause button on your CD player to allow pupils longer to respond to the longer phrases. At the end of each story there are a few questions to check how well children remember the French words and phrases used.

Logos used in the book

The following logos have been used to make it easier for you to locate appropriate activities:

 As role play is such an excellent way of giving children the opportunity to practise speaking French, we have highlighted where opportunities for this occur.

 This logo indicates that a photocopiable sheet is required. Some of the sheets are designed to be cut out and used as flashcards. To make these more attractive, they could be coloured in (either by you or the children). Laminating will increase their durability.

 This logo indicates that a track on one of the CDs is required.

 The musical notes logo indicates that a song is being suggested.

Bonjour

Learning objective
* To greet different people

Vocabulaire	Vocabulary
bonjour	hello
madame	madam
mademoiselle	miss
monsieur	mister/sir
au revoir	good bye
la classe	the class

Resources needed
* Sheets 1a and 1b (pages 9–10)
* Globe (optional)
* CD1, Track 1: Marvin starts his adventure
* *J'aime Chanter!* (optional)

Recap

 Start by finding out any French that the children know. Some may have picked up some French from older siblings. Look at France on a map of Europe (Sheet 1a) or on a globe. Ask if any of the children have been to France. Discuss how they travelled there and what they saw.

Introducing the vocabulary

Say 'Bonjour la classe' to the group and explain that they should all reply together 'Bonjour madame' (if you are a woman) or 'Bonjour monsieur' (if you are a man). They should repeat after you several times. I've found that children love repeating together.

Introduce the terms 'Bonjour mademoiselle' and 'Bonjour monsieur' (if not already introduced). Explain that to each other they should say, 'Bonjour mademoiselle' to girls and 'Bonjour monsieur' to boys.

Pupils should repeat all three phrases after you several times.

Explain that in France it is traditional to greet people either with kisses on the cheek or with a handshake. They will probably be surprised by this.

Shake hands with individual pupils using the phrases, and wait for them to reply.

Activities

 Ask the children to move around the room greeting each other in French using 'Bonjour mademoiselle/monsieur'. They can shake hands if they wish.

Pairs of children can demonstrate their conversation in front of the class. Children usually love being chosen to do this.

 Extend the conversation by using 'Au revoir'. Ask pupils to repeat it after you several times, then add it to their conversations, moving around the class. Ask pairs to demonstrate this afterwards.

1b Give each child a copy of Sheet 1b. Let pupils colour in the finger puppets. Cut along the lines, then glue the puppets together, following the instructions on the sheet. Use them to have simple conversations using 'Bonjour monsieur,' 'Bonjour mademoiselle' and 'Au revoir.'

Say 'Au revoir la classe' at the end of your time with them. Wave at the same time to reinforce the meaning.

Song idea

The first verse of 'Bonjour' in *J'aime Chanter!* uses the vocabulary is this lesson, with the addition of 'À bientôt' (which means 'see you soon'). The second verse introduces 'Salut' ('Hi').

CD story

Listen to Track 1 on CD1: Marvin starts his adventure. Encourage pupils to practise the French phrases in the pauses. The story links nicely to the initial discussion in the lesson, about what the children know about France, and how to get there.

Where is France?

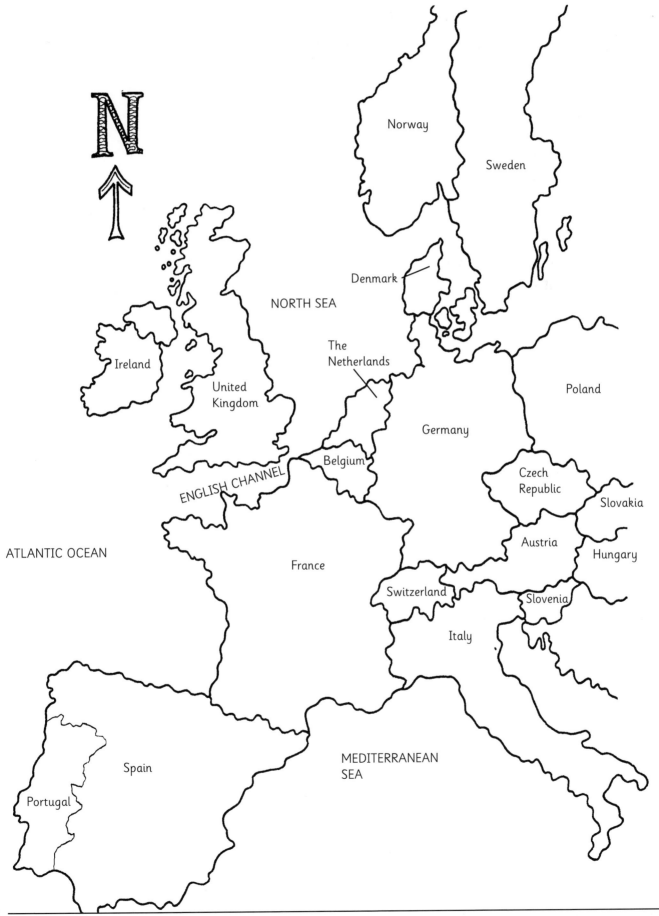

N

Norway

Sweden

Denmark

NORTH SEA

The
Netherlands

Poland

Ireland

United
Kingdom

Germany

Belgium

Czech
Republic

Slovakia

ENGLISH CHANNEL

ATLANTIC OCEAN

Austria

Hungary

France

Switzerland

Slovenia

Italy

Spain

MEDITERRANEAN
SEA

Portugal

Bonjour!

Instructions

∗   Colour in the puppets.

∗   Carefully cut along the dotted line.

∗   Glue on the reverse side in the shaded areas only (see fig. 1).

∗   Fold together and put on your finger.

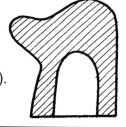

fig. 1

J'aime Parler!
© Ann May and Brilliant Publications

Ça va?

Learning objective
* To ask and talk about how you are

Vocabulaire	Vocabulary
Ça va?	How are you?
ça va bien, merci	I'm fine, thank you
comme ci, comme ça	so-so

Resources needed
* Sheets 2a and 2b (pages 13–14)
* CD1, Track 2: Marvin and Loulou go to the market
* *Chantez Plus Fort!* (optional)

Recap
* Bonjour madame/mademoiselle/monsieur

Introducing the vocabulary
Talk about how you would reply in English when someone asks how you are. With young children it is always a good idea to have a short discussion in English about the lesson subject matter before teaching anything new in French, to avoid any confusion.

Explain that to ask how someone is, you say, 'Ça va?' Pupils should repeat this phrase several times after you.

Explain that if you are feeling well, you say 'Ça va bien, merci.' Stress the importance of using manners here. Use a thumbs up sign to reinforce meaning. Pupils should repeat the phrase several times, perhaps repeating one word at a time at first if they have pronunciation difficulties with the whole phrase.

Pupils should go around the room asking and answering the question in French. Then pairs can demonstrate at the front.

Next, say if you are not sure if you are feeling OK or not, you use 'comme ci, comme ça', Use a flat hand sign to reinforce meaning. Let pupils practise and demonstrate as before.

Activities

Practise conversation in pairs using:
* Bonjour monsieur/mademoiselle
* Ça va?
* Ça va bien, merci
* Comme ci, comme ça
* Au revoir.

Ask pairs to demonstrate the conversation.

Photocopy Sheets 2a and 2b onto card (or stick them onto card) for best results. Let pupils colour in the masks, then cut them out and fasten the masks to sticks. Children can use the masks to practise conversations.

Song idea

The first three verses of 'Bonjour, ça va' in *Chantez Plus Fort!* reinforce the vocabulary introduced in this lesson.

CD story

Listen to Track 2 on CD1: Marvin and Loulou go to the market. Encourage pupils to practise the French phrases in the pauses. If French markets are held near to where you live, you could ask if pupils have ever been to one. What has been on sale? How are they different from UK markets they have visited?

Ça va bien

Comme ci, comme ça

Ça ne va pas

Learning objective
* To ask and talk about how you are (continued)
* To recognize the French flag

Vocabulaire	Vocabulary
ça ne va pas	I'm not so well
ça va mal	I'm ill

Resources needed
* Picture of French flag
* Sheets 3a–3c (pages 17–19)
* *Chantez Plus Fort!* (optional)
* CD1, Track 3: Marvin and Loulou visit Amélie

Recap
* Ça va and responses

Introducing the vocabulary

Explain that sometimes you might not be feeling so good when asked how you are. Then you would say, 'Ça ne va pas'. Demonstrate this with a thumbs down action. Pupils should repeat several times before asking other pupils 'Ça va?' and practising the new answer. Pairs can demonstrate the conversation.

 Explain that if you are injured, in pain or feel sick you should say 'Ça va mal'. Ask pupils to repeat the phrase, holding a part of their body that hurts, then hobble around the room, practising the question and the new answer. The pupils will enjoy pretending to be injured!

Activities

 Practise conversation using:
* Bonjour monsieur/mademoiselle
* Ça va? (Pupils can reply, saying how they really feel this time, using any of the responses learned)
* Au revoir.

 3a Ask if anyone can say or guess the colours on the French flag, then show a picture of the flag. Discuss where they may have seen it, for example, international sporting events on TV or at a visiting French market (if you have one in your area). Allow pupils to colour in the flag on Sheet 3a blue, white and red at their own pace. (Note: the blue stripe is always closest to the flag pole.)

 3b-3c Photocopy Sheets 3b and 3c onto card (or stick them onto card) for best results. Have pupils colour in the masks, then cut them out and fasten the masks to sticks. Children can use the masks to practise conversations in conjunction with masks made from Sheets 2a and 2b.

Song idea

 The final three verses of 'Bonjour, ça va' in *Chantez Plus Fort!* reinforce the vocabulary in this lesson. Singing the whole song will reinforce vocabulary learned in Lesson 2.

CD story

 Listen to Track 3 on CD1: Marvin and Loulou visit Amélie. Encourage pupils to practise the French phrases in the pauses.

Le drapeau français

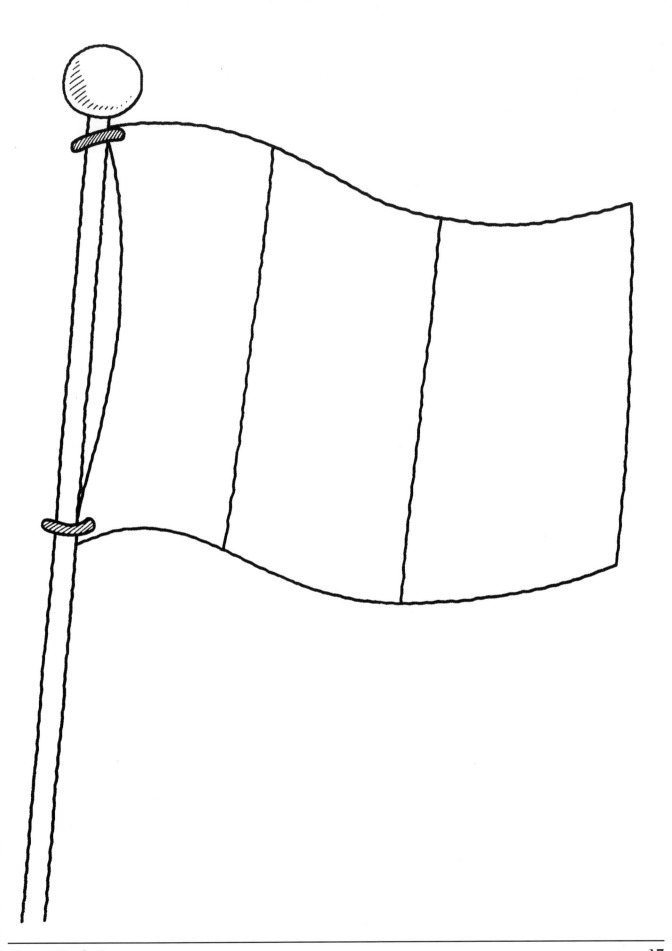

Ça ne va pas

Ça va mal

Je m'appelle ...

Learning objective
* To ask and say your name
* To say yes and no

Vocabulaire	Vocabulary
Comment t'appelles-tu?	What's your name?
Je m'appelle …	My name is …
oui	yes
non	no

Resources needed
* Sheet 4a (page 22)
* Pictures of famous people
* CD1, Track 4: Marvin and Loulou go to the playground

Recap
* Ça va and responses

Introducing the vocabulary

Say you are going to ask pupils what their names are. Use 'Comment t'appelles-tu?' Pupils repeat the question several times. Then say, 'Je m'appelle (your name).' Pupils then repeat 'Je m'appelle …' with their own names. Ask the question, then listen to individuals reply.

 Pupils go around the class, asking and answering the question. Then ask pairs of children to demonstrate their work.

Explain that 'oui' means 'yes' and 'non' means 'no'. Use head movements to reinforce the meaning.

Activities

Say 'Je m'appelle Fred.' Pupils reply 'Non!' Pupils reply 'Oui!' when you say your correct name. A pupil could then come to the front and play this game with the class.

Pupils sit in a circle and ask and answer the question around the circle, while everybody listens.

Pupils could pretend to be someone famous, eg 'Je m'appelle Prince Charles.' Use pictures of famous people as prompts.

 Role-play people meeting in different situations, eg meeting someone new at a playground (as in the CD story), or while on holiday in France.

 On Sheet 4a, pupils fill in their name and draw a self-portrait. Alternatively, they could fill in someone else's name and draw that person.

4a

CD story

Listen to Track 4 on CD1: Marvin and Loulou go to the playground. Encourage pupils to practise the French phrases in the pauses.

Je m'appelle _____.

C'est combien?

Learning objective
* To count to 12

Resources needed
* Number flashcards
* Sheets 5a–5c (pages 25–27)
* CD1, Track 5: Marvin and Loulou go to the café
* CD2, Track 10: '1, 2, 3 nous irons au bois' (instrumental version: CD2, Track 11)
* *Chantez Plus Fort!* and *J'aime Chanter!* (optional)

Vocabulaire	Vocabulary
Et toi?	And you?
C'est combien?	How much is it?
un	one
deux	two
trois	three
quatre	four
cinq	five
six	six
sept	seven
huit	eight
neuf	nine
dix	ten
onze	eleven
douze	twelve

Recap
* Comment t'appelles-tu? Je m'appelle …

Introducing the vocabulary
Tell the pupils you are going to count to three in French. Use fingers for counting. Ask pupils to repeat several times. Do the same with the next three numbers and continue in this way until you have reached the number 12. You may wish to spend several short sessions doing this, rather than trying to teach all 12 numbers in one go.

Use number flashcards, in random order, to test knowledge of individual numbers. Ask the children 'C'est combien?'

Activities
Count forwards and backwards in French with pupils.

In pairs pupils practise counting as far as they can, then demonstrate their counting individually or in pairs.

 On Sheet 5a encourage the pupils to say the numbers as they colour them in. Alternatively, you could say the numbers in a random order, for the pupils to colour in.

Song ideas
 Teach the French song, '1, 2, 3 nous irons au bois', using Track 10 on CD2:

1, 2, 3 nous irons au bois,	*1, 2, 3 We are going to the woods*
4, 5, 6, cueillir des cerises	*4, 5, 6 to pick some cherries*
7, 8, 9 dans mon panier neuf	*7, 8, 9 in my new basket.*
10, 11, 12 elles seront toutes rouges.	*10, 11, 12 They will be all red.*

Explain the meaning of the song. Flashcards made from Sheets 5b–5c or real objects, could be used to teach the vocabulary first (colour in the picture for 'rouge' on Sheet 5c in red). When all the children have learned the song, they could act it out as they sing.

 The rap 'Comptons jusqu'a 20' in *J'aime Chanter!* is great for teaching the numbers (use just the first verse at this stage). Another good song to try is 'Nous allons compter (Partie A)' in *Chantez Plus Fort!* Children love the section when you count down the number of apples in the basket to find the caterpillar!

CD story

Listen to Track 5 on CD1: Marvin and Loulou go the café. Encourage pupils to practise the French phrases in the pauses. You could talk about how French cafés often have tables outside, with parasols to shade people from the sun.

C'est combien?

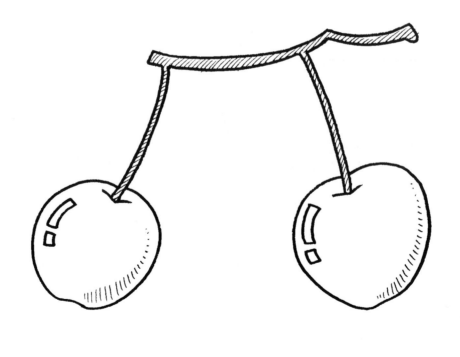

J'aime Parler!
© Ann May and Brilliant Publications

J'ai ... ans

Learning objective

✳ To ask and talk about your age

Vocabulaire	Vocabulary
Quel âge as-tu?	How old are you?
J'ai … ans	I'm … years old

Resources needed

✳ Sheet 6a (page 30)

✳ Number flashcards

✳ CD1, Track 6: Marvin and Loulou visit the school

✳ *Chantez Plus Fort!* and *J'aime Chanter!* (optional)

Recap

✳ C'est combien?

✳ Numbers to 12

Introducing the vocabulary

Tell the children they are going to learn to say how old they are in French. Ask them to say the number of their age first of all, eg cinq. Then ask all the 5-year-olds to say 'J'ai cinq ans' and all the 6-year-olds to say 'J'ai six ans' and so on, according to their ages. Repeat several times, then ask the class to tell the people near them how old they are in French.

Next tell the class they are going to learn to ask how old someone is. Say 'Quel âge as-tu?' asking the children to repeat several times. Ask the question to individuals, then get the children to ask the question to the people around them.

Activities

Say the sentence with different ages in it, eg 'J'ai dix ans' and pupils raise their hand or stand up when the hear their own age.

Sit or stand in a circle and say 'J'ai … ans' around the class.

 Get children to practise the question and answer with a partner, then go and ask other children in the class.

 Practise conversation learned so far with different people in the class:

✳ Bonjour mademoiselle/monsieur

✳ Ça va (and responses)

✳ Comment t'appelles-tu?

✳ Je m'appelle …

✳ Quel âge as-tu?

✳ J'ai … ans.

On Sheet 6a, ask the children to add in the correct number of candles for their own age on the cake, then colour in the picture. Alternatively, you could call out a number in French and the pupils can draw in the right number of candles.

Song ideas

'Quel âge as-tu?' from *J'aime Chanter!* and 'Quel âge as-tu?' from *Chantez Plus Fort!* are both good songs for reinforcing 'Quel âge as-tu?' and numbers to 12. Encourage pupils to sing the songs (possibly with the 'karaoke' backing), using their own name and age.

CD story

Listen to Track 6 on CD1: Marvin and Loulou visit the school. Encourage pupils to practise the French phrases in the pauses.

J'ai _____ ans

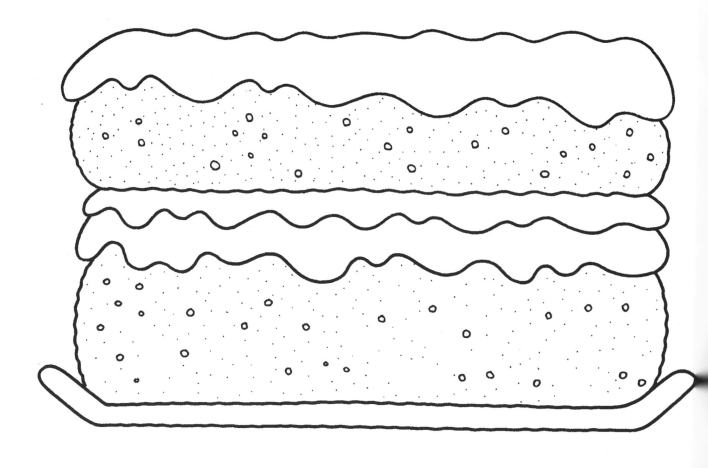

J'aime Parler!
© Ann May and Brilliant Publications

L'alphabet

Learning objective
✳   To say the alphabet

Resources needed
✳   Sheet 7a (page 33)
✳   Alphabet cards
✳   CD1, Track 7: Marvin learns the alphabet
✳   *Chantez Plus Fort!* and *J'aime Chanter!* (optional)

Vocabulaire	Vocabulary
Comment ça s'écrit?	How do I write that?

Recap
✳   Quel âge as-tu?
✳   J'ai … ans

Introducing the vocabulary
Pupils repeat the alphabet several times. The alphabet could be taught in sections or the vowels could be taught first. Point out that 'i' and 'j' rhyme.

Ask pupils to repeat the whole alphabet and pay special attention to the letters in their first name.

Show alphabet cards at random and pupils have to say the letter in French.

Revise 'Comment t'appelles-tu?' then ask 'Comment ça s'écrit?', explaining that you are now asking how their name is spelt. As a response the children should spell out their first names, eg:
✳   Comment t'appelles-tu?
✳   Je m'appelle Louise
✳   Comment ça s'écrit?
✳   L O U I S E

Activities

Practise 'Comment t'appelles-tu?' and 'Comment ça s'écrit?' in pairs. Then ask others in the class. Ask pairs to demonstrate.

Practise conversations known so far. To make the role-play more realistic, pupils could pretend to be visiting the doctor or dentist, as in the CD story: Marvin learns the alphabet. The receptionist has to ask 'Comment t'appelles-tu?' and 'Comment ça s'écrit?' Patients could reply with their own names, or made-up names.

Play hangman in French, using children's names as the words to work out. Children call out the letters in French.

On Sheet 7a, pupils colour in the letters saying the name of each letter in French as they colour them. Alternatively, pupils could colour each letter in as the teachers calls them out in French, or colour in the letters in their name.

Song ideas

'L'alphabet français' on *J'aime Chanter!* uses the traditional English tune. 'Comment sa s'écrit?' on *Chantez Plus Fort!* has an original, but very catchy, tune. As the title implies, the song reinforces not only pronounciation of the alphabet, but also the phrase, 'Comment ça s'écrit?'

CD story

Listen to Track 7 on CD1: Marvin learns the alphabet. Encourage pupils to practise the French phrases in the pauses.

L'alphabet

a b c d

e f g h

i j k l

m n o p

q r s t

u v w x

y z

C'est la France

Learning objective

* To revise and increase knowledge of France
* To revise conversations

Vocabulaire	Vocabulary
La France	France

Resources needed

* Sheet 8a (page 36)
* Maps of France
* Books about France and/or French artists
* Samples of French cheese, if available
* Samples of French perfume, if available
* CD1, Track 8: Marvin and Loulou go to the supermarket
* Sheet 1a (optional)

Recap

* Alphabet
* What the children already know about France

Introducing the vocabulary

 Look at France and its surrounding countries and seas in greater detail (see Sheet 1a). Explain that when the French refer to their country, France, they say 'La France'.

Discuss different means of transport that can be to used to travel to France (eg boat, plane, train, tunnel, etc).

Discuss things that France is famous for eg cheese, such as Brie, Camembert; perfume such as those made by Dior and Chanel; artists like Monet, Dégas and Rodin.

Activities

Pupils could sample some French cheese, smell some French perfume and/or look at works of French artists in books or on the Internet.

Make collages of things that come from France using pictures cut out of advertisements. Use these to make a display, together with actual items/packaging. Pupils could be encouraged to bring in things from home/holiday to add to the display.

 Revise all the questions and answers learned so far. Pupils go round the room, asking other pupils questions:

* Ça va?
* Comment t'appelles-tu?
* Comment ça s'écrit?
* Quel âge as-tu?

Ask pairs to demonstrate questions and answers.

8a On sheet 8a, pupils can colour in the map of France. Encourage them to add details, eg if they have been on holiday in France they could draw pictures of where they stayed, or things they noticed that were different about France.

CD story

Listen to Track 8 on CD1: Marvin and Loulou go to the supermarket. Encourage pupils to practise the French phrases in the pauses.

La France

Joyeux Noël!

Learning objective

* To celebrate Christmas festivities

Resources needed

* Sheets 9a–9d (pages 39–42)

* CD1, Track 9: Marvin and Loulou celebrate Christmas

* CD2, Track 12: 'Vive le vent' (instrumental version: CD2, Track 13)

* *J'aime Chanter!* (optional)

Vocabulaire	Vocabulary
Joyeux Noël	Merry Christmas
Père Noël	Father Christmas
les grands sapins	the great pine trees
la neige	the snow
les boules de neige	snowballs
les bois	the woods
les champs	the fields

Recap

* All conversations so far

* Bonjour, ça va?

* Comment t'appelles-tu? Comment ça s'écrit?

* Quel âge as-tu?

Introducing the vocabulary

9a Discuss how Christmas is celebrated in France. Children put their shoes in front of the fireplace, so that Père Noël (Father Christmas) can fill them with gifts. Père Noël is usually depicted wearing a long, red, hooded robe edged with white fur. He carries presents in a basket, or *hotte*, like those carried by grape harvesters (see illustration on Sheet 9a). French people decorate their homes with nativity scenes.

Get children to repeat the phrase 'Joyeux Noël' until they can say it to a partner.

9a–9c Make flashcards out of Sheets 9a–9c to teach the vocabulary used in the song 'Vive le Vent' (introduced below and in the CD story: Marvin and Loulou celebrate Christmas).

Activity

9d Pupils can colour in the picture on Sheet 9d. They could cut out the picture and stick it on card to make a calendar or Christmas card.

Song ideas

♪ Learn the traditional French song: 'Vive le Vent', using Track 12 on CD2. Hold up flashcards made from Sheets 9a–9c at the appropriate time.

Vive le vent, vive le vent	*Hooray for the wind, hooray for the wind*
Vive le vent d'hiver	*Hooray for the winter wind*
Qui s'en va, sifflant, soufflant	*That whistles and blows*
Dans les grands sapins verts.	*Through the great, green pine trees.*

Oh! Vive le vent, vive le vent	*Oh! Hooray for the wind, hooray for the wind*
Vive le vent d'hiver	*Hooray for the winter wind*
Boules de neige et Jour de l'An	*Snowballs and New Year's Day*
Et Bonne Année Grand-mère!	*And Happy New Year Grandmother!*
Notre beau cheval blanc,	*Our lovely white horse,*
S'élance sur la neige,	*Rushes through the snow,*
Glissant comme une flèche	*Sliding like an arrow,*
Par les bois et par les champs.	*Through the woods and fields.*
Tout autour du harnais	*All around the harness,*
S'agitent les clochettes	*Little bells are ringing,*
Nous partons à la fête,	*We're off to the party,*
Bonne Année! chantons gaiement.	*Happy New Year, let's gaily sing.*

You may wish to teach just the chorus and save the verses for another lesson, or even for the following year!

Ask the children to repeat the first two lines until known. They should find this quite easy. The rest of the chorus should be broken up into small sections and learned.

 J'aime Chanter! has two additional French Christmas songs. 'Père Noël' is a simple song, sung to the tune of 'Frère Jacques', all about Father Christmas. 'Mon beau sapin' is a traditional French song.

CD story

 Listen to Track 9 on CD2: Marvin and Loulou celebrate Christmas. Encourage pupils to practise the French phrases in the pauses.

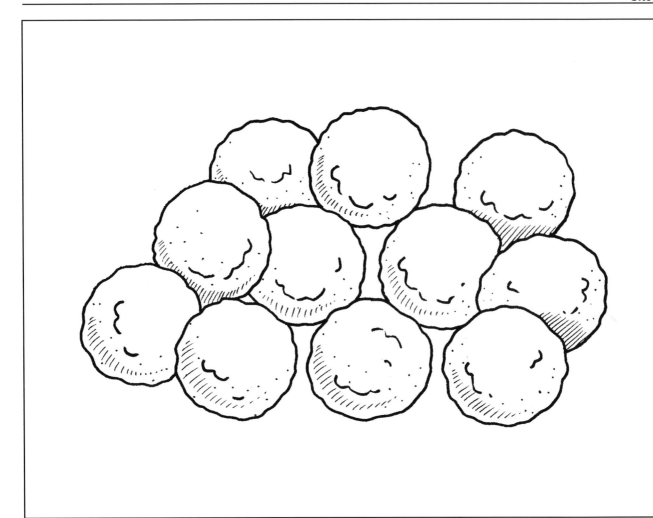

J'aime Parler!
© Ann May and Brilliant Publications

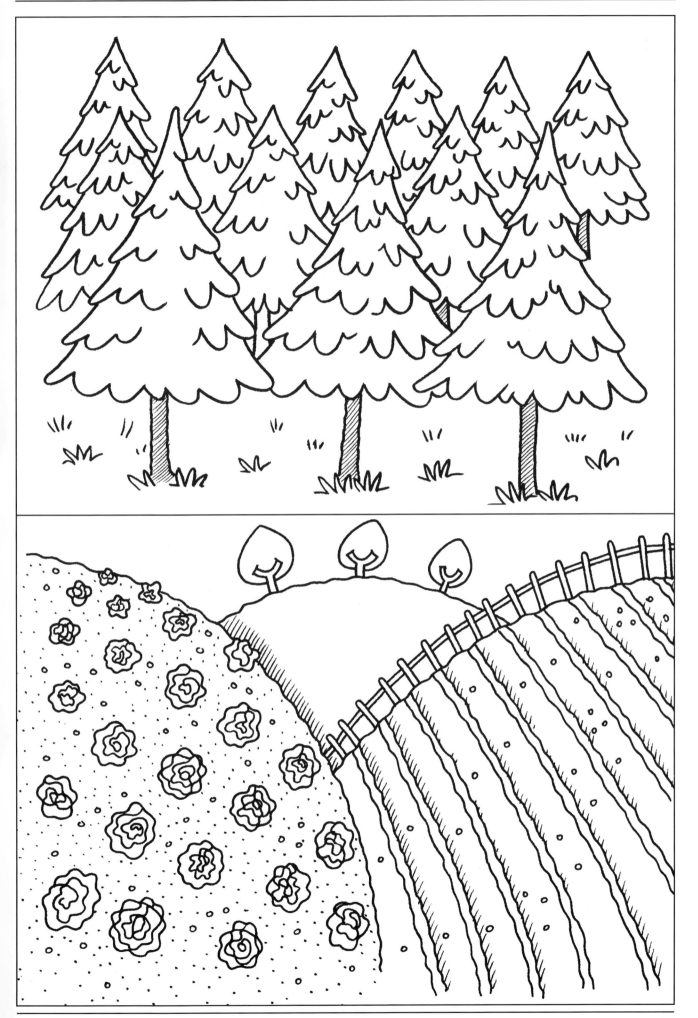

Joyeux Noël!

J'aime Parler!
© Ann May and Brilliant Publications

Bonne Année!

Learning objective
* To continue with Christmas festivities
* To celebrate the new year

Vocabulaire	Vocabulary
Bonne Année	Happy New Year
Vive les vacances	Long live the holidays

Resources
* Sheet 10a (page 44)
* CD1, Track 10: Amélie's New Year's Eve party
* French Christmas DVD/Video (optional)
* DVD/Video player (optional)

Recap
* Joyeux Noël
* Vive le vent song

Introducing the vocabulary
Introduce the term 'Bonne Année' and let children practise saying it to each other. Then introduce 'Vive les vacances'.

Pupils could pretend to be friends, meeting in the street, around Christmas time. Role-play conversations using 'Ça va?' as well as 'Joyeux Noël', 'Bonne Année' and 'Vive les vacances'.

Activities
Sit in a circle. Go round the circle with each child saying 'Joyeux Noël' and the name of the person sitting next to them.

Take turns to stand up and say 'Bonne Année', like a Mexican wave, around the class.

If you can, show a French Christmas DVD/Video (see Resources, page 104). Explain the story in English first and help pupils to understand the meaning throughout the DVD/video. The children will be excited that they have watched a real French DVD/video.

Fold Sheet 10a in half so that the words are on the inside. Pupils can design their own front for the card. Pupils could address the card to a family member and take it home.

CD story

Listen to Track 10 on CD1: Amélie's New Year's Eve party. Encourage pupils to practise the French phrases in the pauses.

Pupils could pretend to be the kittens in the story (either acting themselves, or using cat puppets), and have a conversation.

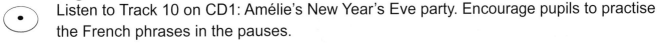

Sheet 10a

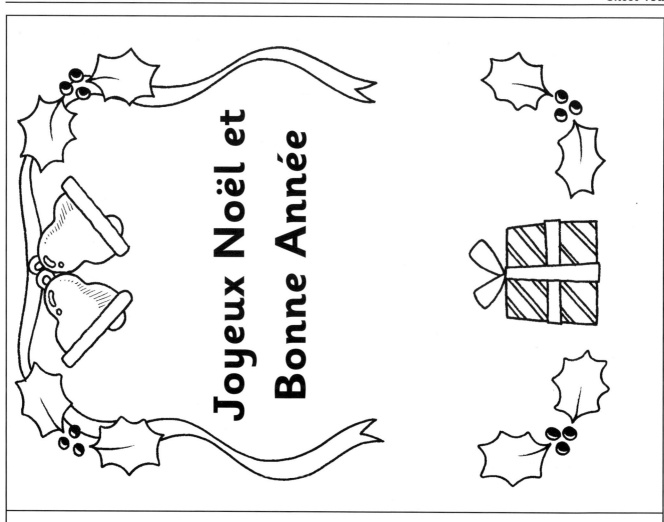

J'aime Parler!
© Ann May and Brilliant Publications

Les jours de la semaine

Learning objective
* To understand and say the days of the week

Resources needed
* Sheet 11a (page 47)
* CD1, Track 11: Marvin and Loulou plan an exciting week
* White/black board for writing on
* *J'aime Chanter!* and *Chantez Plus Fort!* (optional)

<table>
<tr><th>Vocabulaire</th><th>Vocabulary</th></tr>
<tr><td>lundi</td><td>Monday</td></tr>
<tr><td>mardi</td><td>Tuesday</td></tr>
<tr><td>mercredi</td><td>Wednesday</td></tr>
<tr><td>jeudi</td><td>Thursday</td></tr>
<tr><td>vendredi</td><td>Friday</td></tr>
<tr><td>samedi</td><td>Saturday</td></tr>
<tr><td>dimanche</td><td>Sunday</td></tr>
<tr><td>les jours de la semaine</td><td>the days of the week</td></tr>
</table>

Recap
* Previous conversations learned

Introducing the vocabulary
First get the pupils to chant the days of the week in English.

Write on the board the first letter of each day in French, starting with 'lundi' (Monday): l, m, m, j, v, s, d. The pupils should then repeat the days after you. Remind them of how to say each day in English as you go. Do this activity several times.

Then, pointing at the letters, get the pupils to say the words with you.

Activities
Ask children what day of the week they were born on. If they know, they should tell you in French. Some children may have to find out the day of the week they were born on for homework.

You say the days of the week in sequence, missing out one day, which the children then have to fill in. The children love it when they guess the correct day.

You say the days in French and individuals volunteer to mime an activity that they do on that given day, eg swimming. The activities and the days on which they occur could be discussed in English first, so that children can share their enthusiasm for their hobbies and activities.

 Give the pupils Sheet 11a. Tell the pupils the meaning of the title, 'Les jours de la semaine', then ask them to repeat it several times. Then ask them to repeat each day as you point to it on the sheet. Pupils could draw an activity they do for each day of the week.

Alternatively, Sheet 11a can be cut up into cards for the children to put into the correct sequence. The cards could be also used to play pairs and matching games.

Song ideas

Children generally love singing simple rhymes in French. 'Les jours de la semaine' in *J'aime Chanter!* has a simple tune, or you could make up your own.

'Voici les sept jours de la semaine' in *Chantez Plus Fort!* is another good song, although you may find the singing on the CD goes too fast for young children. The tune is very catchy and easy to pick up, so it's easy to sing it unaccompanied.

CD story

Listen to Track 11 on CD1: Marvin and Loulou plan an exciting week. Encourage pupils to practise the French phrases in the pauses.

Les jours de la semaine

lundi	mardi
mercredi	jeudi
vendredi	samedi
dimanche	

Les mois de l'an

Learning objective

*   To understand and say the months of the year

Resources needed

*   Sheet 12a (page 50)
*   CD1, Track 12: Loulou teaches Marvin a rhyme
*   White/black board for writing on
*   French months of the year poster (for suppliers see Useful Resources page 104)
*   CD2, Track 14: Les mois de l'an (instrumental version: CD2, Track 15)

Vocabulaire	Vocabulary
janvier	January
février	February
mars	March
avril	April
mai	May
juin	June
juillet	July
août	August
septembre	September
octobre	October
novembre	November
décembre	December
les mois de l'an	the months of the year

Recap

*   Days of the week

Introducing the vocabulary

Ask the children to chant the months of the year in English first of all.

 Show pupils a poster of the months of the year in French (Sheet 12a could be enlarged if no French poster is available).

Pupils repeat each month. Do this several times until the pupils can say the months with you.

Activities

Say each month in turn. Pupils put up their hands when they hear their birthday month.

Pupils say the month in which they were born in French (find out for homework if necessary, or find out for them from office records).

Make a chart of birthdays on the whiteboard. Have the months written out and put pupils names under their birthday month. Then, say the months in turn and the pupils have to stand up as soon as they hear their own birthday month.

 Let pupils colour in Sheet 12a. Alternatively, the months can be cut up for pupils to arrange in the correct order, or for snap and matching games.

Song ideas

Teach the song, 'Les mois de l'an' using Track 14 on CD2 (sung to the tune of 'Au clair de la lune'). The third line of the song uses the phrase, 'Vive les vacances', which was introduced in Lesson 10.

Janvier, février, mars, avril, mai, juin
Juillet, août, septembre, octobre, novembre
Décembre, Noël, vive les vacances.
Janvier, février, mars, avril, mai, juin.

Alternatively, you could use 'Les mois de 'l'an' in *J'aime Chanter!*

CD story

Listen to Track 12 on CD1: Loulou teaches Marvin a rhyme. Encourage pupils to practise the French phrases in the pauses.

© Ann May and Brilliant Publications

Les mois

J'aime Parler!
© Ann May and Brilliant Publications

Les nombres 13–31

Learning objective
* To count from 13 to 31

Resources needed
* Sheet 13a (page 53)
* Number chart
* Number flashcards
* Classroom items to count
* CD1, Track 13: Marvin and Loulou go to the toy shop
* *J'aime Chanter!* (optional)

Recap
* Numbers 1–12
* Months

Introducing the vocabulary
Teach 13–16 first, then numbers 17–19. Numbers 20 to 31 will be easier to learn. You may need to spend two lessons on learning the numbers.

Looking at a number chart, say all the numbers up to 31 in French. Count forwards and backwards.

Use number flashcards, in random order, to test knowledge of individual numbers. Ask the children, 'C'est combien?'

Vocabulaire	Vocabulary
treize	thirteen
quatorze	fourteen
quinze	fifteen
seize	sixteen
dix-sept	seventeen
dix-huit	eighteen
dix-neuf	nineteen
vingt	twenty
vingt et un	twenty one
vingt-deux	twenty two
vingt-trois	twenty three
vingt-quatre	twenty four
vingt-cinq	twenty five
vingt-six	twenty six
vingt-sept	twenty seven
vingt-huit	twenty eight
vingt-neuf	twenty nine
trente	thirty
trente et un	thirty one
un chat	a cat

Activities
Count items in the room, eg scissors, pencils, books, etc. Hold up the items (or point to them) and ask, 'C'est combien?'

Count in twos, forwards and backwards.

13a   On Sheet 13a, pupils can colour in the animals and write the number. Encourage them to count in French, pointing at each item.

In pairs, children practise counting as far as they can, then demonstrate their counting individually or in pairs.

Song idea

 Use the rap 'Comptons jusqu'a 20' from *J'aime Chanter!* to practise and reinforce the numbers to 20.

CD story

 Listen to Track 13 on CD1: Marvin and Loulou go to the toy shop. Encourage pupils to practise the French phrases in the pauses. The story introduces the word, 'un chat' (a cat). More animals are introduced in the Lessons 15 and 16.

C'est combien?

Bon anniversaire

Learning objective
* To ask and talk about your birthday
* To understand and say dates

Vocabulaire	Vocabulary
Mon anniversaire est le …	My birthday is …
Quelle est la date de ton anniversaire?	When is your birthday?
Quelle est la date?	What is the date?
bon anniversaire	happy birthday

Resources needed
* Sheet 14a (page 56)
* CD1, Track 14: Marvin and Loulou go to Amélie's birthday party
* *J'aime Chanter!* and *Chantez Plus Fort!* (optional)

Recap
* Numbers 1–31
* Months

Introducing the vocabulary

Tell the pupils you are going to ask them when their birthdays are in French: 'Quelle est la date de ton anniversaire?' Make notes on when their birthdays are (or have office records available so that you can help them). Help pupils to say the number and month of their birthday in French. Stress that the number always comes before the month in French.

Progress to 'Mon anniversaire est le … .' The children will find this much more difficult.

Activities

Pupils can practise asking and answering the question, 'Quelle est la date de ton anniversaire?' in pairs.

Discuss what today's date is in English. Tell the class the date in French and write it on the board. Introduce 'Quelle est la date?' and invite the answer in French.

Work out the dates for yesterday and tomorrow in French with the children. Say them and write them on the board.

Identify important dates to the children, discussing their significance in English first, eg 25 décembre, 14 février, 31 octobre. Say the dates in French and write them on the board.

 Let pupils colour in Sheet 14a. They could also write their birthday in French at the bottom of the sheet.

Song ideas

Sing 'Bon anniversaire' in French, using the same tune as 'Happy birthday to you'. Children will find this very easy:

Bon anniversaire, bon anniversaire
Bon anniversaire, bon anniversaire

Quel âge as-tu? in *J'aime Chanter!* and 'Quelle est la date?' in *Chantez Plus Fort!* are both excellent songs for reinforcing the vocabulary introduced in this lesson.

CD story

Listen to Track 14 on CD1: Marvin and Loulou go to Amélie's birthday party. Encourage pupils to practise the French phrases in the pauses.

Bon anniversaire

Mon anniversaire est

le _____ _____ .

Qu'est ce que c'est?

Learning objective

* To understand and say some animal vocabulary
* To learn to use and respond to 'Qu'est ce que c'est?'

Resources needed

* Sheets 15a–15c (pages 59–61)
* CD2, Track 1: Marvin and Loulou go to the pet shop
* *J'aime Chanter!* (optional)

Vocabulaire	Vocabulary
Qu'est ce que c'est?	What is this?
c'est	it is/it's
un chat	a cat
un chien	a dog
un lapin	a rabbit
un hamster	a hamster
un poisson	a fish
une gerbille	a gerbil
ou	or

Recap

* Dates for birthdays and other important events

Introducing the vocabulary

Ask children the question, 'Qu'est ce que c'est?' and ask the children to repeat it several times.

 Hold up one of the animal flashcards (made from Sheets 15a–15c) and say, eg 'C'est un chat' several times. Do the same with the other flashcards.

Show the cat flashcard and ask 'C'est un lapin? Oui ou non?' The pupils say 'Non' together. They do this until you say 'C'est un chat?' when they should respond with 'Oui' together.

Now give the children a choice. Hold up the cat flashcard and ask 'C'est un lapin ou un chat?' Invite answers from individuals. Repeat this method with the other flashcards.

Finally ask, 'Qu'est ce que c'est?' for each flashcard.

The pupils will love learning the names of animals in French.

The above method can be used for teaching any new vocabulary when the question is 'Qu'est ce que c'est?'

Activities

 Hide a flashcard (made from Sheets 15a–15c) so that pupils can't see it and they guess which animal it is in French.

Pupils take turns to mime an animal and the other pupils guess which one it is. Encourage them to answer with, 'C'est … .'

Do a survey of which pets the children have in French. If they do not know the French for their pet, let them say it in English. Make a note of any other pets the children have for the next lesson. Make or find flashcards of these for next time.

 If you would like to give pupils a colouring activity, they could colour in some of the flashcard pictures (Sheets 15a–15c).

Song idea

 The song, 'Les animaux' on *J'aime Chanter!* uses many of these animals, in addition to other common pets and farm animals.

CD story

 Listen to Track 1 on CD2: Marvin and Loulou go to the pet shop. Encourage pupils to practise the French phrases in the pauses.

J'aime Parler!
© Ann May and Brilliant Publications

Tu as ... ? J'ai ...

Learning objective

✳   To understand and say some animal vocabulary

✳   To learn to ask 'Tu as ... ?' and respond 'J'ai ... '

Vocabulaire	Vocabulary
Tu as ... ?	Do you have ... ?
j'ai ...	I have ...
un oiseau	a bird
un cheval	a horse

(and other pets depending on what the children have)

Resources needed

✳   Sheets 16a–16b (pages 64–65)

✳   CD2, Track 2: Marvin and Loulou go for a walk

✳   Sheets 15a–15c (pages 59–61)

Recap

✳   Qu'est ce que c'est?

✳   C'est un chat/ chien/ lapin/ hamster/ poisson

Introducing the vocabulary

 Teach the new animal vocabulary using the same method as in Lesson 15. Use flashcards made from Sheet 16a.

The children should then repeat 'Tu as un animal?' several times. Tell them what the question means.

 Go through all the animals flashcards (made from Sheets 15a–15c and 16a) with the children repeating 'J'ai …' for each one. Then they should only repeat for the pets that they own.

Activities

 Pupils go around the room asking and answering the question. Pairs can demonstrate this afterwards.

 Include the question and answer in general conversation learned so far:

✳   Bonjour, ça va?

✳   Comment t'appelles-tu? Comment ça s'écrit?

✳   Quel âge as tu?

✳   Quelle est la date de ton anniversaire?

✳   Tu as un animal?

 Hide one of the flashcards so that pupils can't see it and they have to guess which animal it is in French.

Pairs can demonstrate all the conversation they can remember.

Pupils take turns to mime an animal and the other pupils guess which one it is. Encourage them to answer with, 'C'est …'.

 On Sheet 16b, pupils can draw a pet they have or one they would like to own.

Song idea

 The song, 'Les animaux' on *J'aime Chanter!* uses many of these animals, in addition to other common pets and farm animals.

CD story

 Listen to Track 2 on CD2: Marvin and Loulou go for a walk. Encourage pupils to practise the French phrases in the pauses.

J'aime Parler!
© Ann May and Brilliant Publications

J'ai _____

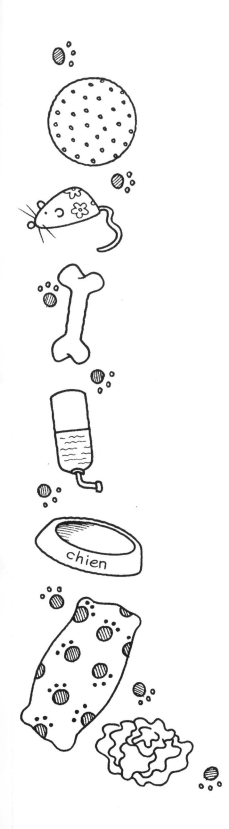

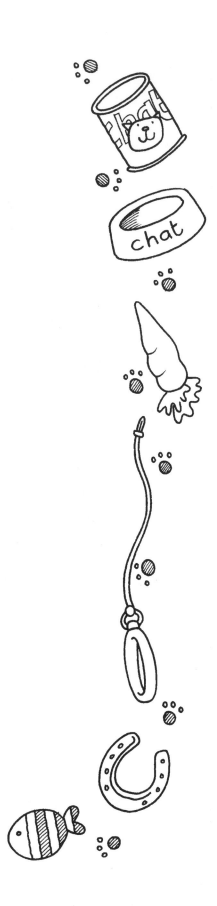

Mes frères et mes sœurs

Learning objective

* To ask and say if you have a brother or sister

Vocabulaire	Vocabulary
un frère	a brother
une sœur	a sister
très	very

Resources

* Sheet 17a (page 68)
* CD2, Track 3: Marvin and Loulou visit a farm
* White/black board for writing on
* *J'aime Chanter!* (optional)

Recap

* Tu as un animal?

Introducing the vocabulary

Draw a matchstick picture of yourself on the board, with a brother and a sister beside you. Alternatively, you could use photos of your real siblings.

Point to the brother and say, 'J'ai un frère'. The pupils should repeat this several times.

Point to the sister and say, 'J'ai une sœur'. The pupils repeat several times again.

Ask 'Tu as un frère?', pointing to the children and the brother picture. Tell the children to reply, 'Oui, j'ai un frère' or 'Non' if they don't. Ask various individuals.

Do the same with 'Tu as une sœur?'

Activities

Do a survey of brothers and sisters. Have a matchstick brother and sister as the headings on the board. Ask 'Tu as un frère? and 'Tu as une sœur?' to each child. See if there are more brothers or sisters belonging to the class. Discuss in English.

Teach 'J'ai deux frères' etc, depending on what the children have. Make notes of what siblings each child has for future reference.

 Pupils go around the rooms asking and answering the questions: 'Tu as un frère? Tu as une sœur?' Pairs can then demonstrate to the class.

 On Sheet 17a, pupils cross out or add until they have the right amount of brothers and sisters on the sheet, then colour in. Pupils without siblings could draw 'mon cousin/ma cousine' (my cousin) or a favourite pet or animal on a blank sheet of paper.

Include the questions and answers in general conversation learned so far:

* Bonjour, ça va?
* Comment t'appelles-tu? Comment ça s'écrit?
* Quel âge as tu?
* Quelle est la date de ton anniversaire?
* Tu as un animal?
* Tu as un frère? Tu as une sœur?

Song idea

 'Ma famille' in *J'aime Chanter!* is a lively, catchy tune for reinforcing names of family members. In addition to sœur and 'frère' it also introduces 'mère', 'père', 'grand-mère', 'grand-père', 'tante', 'oncle', and 'cousin/cousine'.

CD story

 Listen to Track 3 on CD2: Marvin and Loulou visit a farm. Encourage pupils to practise the French phrases in the pauses. A goat and a sheep appear in this story. Here are the French words, in case you'd like to teach them:

un chèvre	a goat
un mouton	a sheep

J'ai _____ frère/frères.

J'ai _____ sœur/sœurs.

J'aime Parler!
© Ann May and Brilliant Publications

Il/Elle s'appelle ...

Learning objective
* To ask and say your brother or sister's name(s)

Resources
* Sheets 18a–18b (pages 71–72)
* Board
* CD2, Track 4: Marvin and Loulou visit the ginger cat family
* *J'aime Chanter!* (optional)

Recap
* Tu as un frère/ une sœur?
* Oui, j'ai un frère/ une sœur.
* J'ai (deux/ trois) frères/ sœurs.

Vocabulaire	Vocabulary
Tu as des frères ou des sœurs?	Do you have any brothers or sister?
Comment s'appelle-t-il?	What's his name?
Comment s'appelle-t-elle?	What's her name?
Il s'appelle …	His name is …
Elle s'appelle …	Her name is …
aussi	also

Introducing the vocabulary

Say that you are going to ask the children if they have any brothers or sisters. Pupils repeat 'Tu as des frères ou des soeurs?' several times.

Ask the question to invidivuals and help them to reply: 'Oui, j'ai un frère' etc. Ask the pupils to say their brothers names using 'Il s'appelle … .' (Use the notes you made of the children's brothers and sisters to help speed up the process!)

Teach 'Elle s'appelle … ' in the same way.

Draw stick figures of yourself and brothers and sisters on the board (or use a photo). Say 'J'ai un frère. J'ai aussi deux sœurs.' Make sure they understand that 'aussi' means 'also'. Let them try using it themselves.

Activities

Pupils with only one brother stand up when you say 'J'ai un frère' etc. Do this with other phrases about siblings.

Write the names of brothers and sisters on the board. Go around the class asking 'Tu as des frères ou des sœurs? Comment s'appelle-t-il/elle? and have a list of brothers and a list of sisters. The children will be delighted to see their siblings' names on the board.

Pupils go around the room asking and answering the question, 'Tu as des frères ou des sœurs?', adding their siblings' names. Pairs can then demonstrate their questions to the class.

On Sheets 18a–18b, pupils draw a picture of a sibling. Pupils with no sibling can make one up or could draw a cousin or a friend on a blank piece of paper instead.

Song idea

'Ma famille' in *J'aime Chanter!* is a lively, catchy tune for reinforcing names of family members. In addition to soeur and 'frère' it also introduces 'mère', 'père', 'grand-mère', 'grand-père', 'tante', 'oncle', and 'cousin/cousine'.

CD story

Listen to Track 4 on CD2: Marvin and Loulou visit the ginger cat family. Encourage pupils to practise the French phrases in the pauses. The story is a lovely starting point for a discussion of French names. Discuss how, although many are spelled the same way as the English equivalent, they are pronounced differently. Here are some common French names. The ones that are asterisked, appear in the CD story.

Girl names
Amélie*
Chloé
Clara
Emma
Inès
Léa
Louise*
Loulou*
Manon
Natalie*

Boy names
Enzo
Hugo
Killian
Lucas
Mathis
Mattéo
Max*
Patrice*
Théo
Thomas*

J'aime Parler!
© Ann May and Brilliant Publications

Mon frère s'appelle

Ma sœur s'appelle

© Ann May and Brilliant Publications

Frère Jacques

Lesson 19

Vocabulaire	Vocabulary
Dormez-vous?	Are you sleeping? (polite)
Sonnez les matinées	Ring the morning bells

Learning objective
* To sing the song 'Frère Jacques'

Resources
* Sheet 19a (page 75)
* CD2, Track 5: Marvin and Loulou go to the beach
* CD2, Track 16: Frère Jacques (instrumental version: CD2, Track 17)

Recap
* Tu as des frères ou des sœurs?
* Oui, j'ai un frère/ une sœur.
* Il/elle s'appelle …

Introducing the vocabulary/song idea
Play the song, 'Frère Jacques' (Track 16 on CD2) for the children to listen to and explain it's meaning in English. Explain that 'frère' is a religious title, so 'Frère Jacques is a monk or friar whose job it is to ring the church bells to call everyone to morning prayers.

Pupils repeat each line of the song after you until they can say them well:

Frère Jacques, Frère Jacques,
Dormez-vous? Dormez-vous?
Sonnez les matinées, sonnez les matinées.

Din dang dong, din dang dong.

Brother John, Brother John,
Are you sleeping? Are you sleeping?
Ring the morning bells. Ring the morning bells.

Ding dang dong, ding dang dong.

Pupils sing each line after you, then sing along with you as soon as they are ready to.

When the song is well known you could divide the class into two groups and sing the song as a round.

Activities
Work out some actions to the song. They could mime sleeping to 'dormez-vous' and ringing a bell to 'sonnez les matinées'.

On Sheet 19a, pupils can colour in the picture illustrating the song.

Pupils go around the room asking and answering questions about brothers and sisters.

J'aime Parler!
© Ann May and Brilliant Publications

73

Revise general conversation. Pairs can then demonstrate their questions to the class:

* Bonjour, ça va?
* Comment t'appelles-tu? Comment ça s'écrit?
* Quel âge as tu?
* Quelle est la date de ton anniversaire?
* Tu as un animal?
* Tu as des frères ou des soeurs?
* Comment s'appelle't-il/elle?

CD story

 Listen to Track 5 on CD2: Marvin and Loulou go to the beach. Encourage pupils to practise the French phrases in the pauses.

Frère Jacques

Ma mère et mon père

Learning objective

* To say what your parents are called

Resources

* Sheet 20a–20b (pages 78–79)
* CD2, Track 6: Marvin and Loulou go to see a play
* CD2, Track 16: Frère Jacques (instrumental version: CD2, Track 17)
* *J'aime Chanter!* (optional)

Vocabulaire	Vocabulary
ma mère	my mother
mon père	my father
Comment s'appelle ta mère?	What's your mother's name?
Comment s'appelle ton père?	What's your father's name?
Chut!	Shhh!

Recap

* Tu as des frères ou des soeurs?
* Frère Jacques song

Introducing the vocabulary

Draw a matchstick family on the board, this time with a mother and father above you on the family tree, and explain who they are in English.

Point to the mother and say, 'ma mère'. The children should repeat this after you several times.

Do the same for 'mon père'.

'Chut!' is introduced in the CD story. Children will enjoy practising using this word!

Activities

Children have to guess the names of other pupils' mums, using 'elle s'appelle … .' Some children will know the names of their friend's mums. Write the names on the board.

Do the same with dads' names, using 'il s'appelle … .'

Pupils go around the room asking and answering questions about parents' names. Get them to repeat 'Comment s'appelle ta mère?' and 'Comment s'appelle ton père?' several times first.

 Revise general conversation. You could let children pretend to have a conversation in an inappropriate place, eg a theatre or cinema. Other children could be fellow members of the audience and say 'Chut!'

On Sheets 20a–20b, pupils draw a picture of their mother and father.

Song ideas

 Continue practising 'Frère Jacques' (CD2, Track 16).

 'Ma famille' in *J'aime Chanter!* is a lively, catchy tune for reinforcing names of family members.

CD story

 Listen to Track 6 on CD2: Marvin and Loulou go to see a play. Encourage pupils to practise the French phrases in the pauses.

Ma mère s'appelle

_____ •

Mon père s'appelle

_____ •

J'habite à ...

Learning objective
✳   To ask and say where you live

<table>
<tr><td colspan="2">Vocabulaire   Vocabulary</td></tr>
</table>

Vocabulaire	**Vocabulary**
Où habites-tu?	Where do you live?
J'habite à …	I live …

Resources
✳   Sheet 21a (page 81)
✳   CD2, Track 7: Marvin and Loulou go to the town square
✳   Map of the United Kingdom
✳   Sheet 8a (page 36)

Recap
✳   Comment s'appelle ta mère/ton père?

Introducing the vocabulary
Study a map of the United Kingdom and show pupils where their town/village is situated.

Tell them you are going to say where you live: 'j'habite à (your town/village).' Pupils should repeat the phrase several times. Check if some pupils live in a different town/village and teach them to say, 'J'habite à (different town/village).

Tell the pupils that to ask where you live you say, 'Où habites-tu?' They should repeat this several times.

Activities
Children sit in a circle and they ask and answer the question around the circle. The first child says, 'Où habites-tu?' and the second child replies, then asks 'Où habites-tu?' to the third child in the circle, and so on.

Pupils say what their relatives/famous people would say.

Look at the map again and decide what children from different towns would say.

21a   On Sheet 21a, pupils draw a picture of their town/village.

CD story
Listen to Track 7 on CD2: Marvin and Loulou go to the town square. Encourage pupils to practise the French phrases in the pauses. Find the places mentioned in the story on the map on Sheet 8a: Calais, Boulogne, Paris, Avignon.

J'habite à

Où habites-tu?

Learning objective

* To ask and say whether you live in a house or a flat

Vocabulaire	Vocabulary
une maison	a house
un appartement	a flat
dans	in

Resources

* Sheet 22a (pages 83)
* CD2, Track 8: Marvin and Loulou go to Paris
* Photos of Paris landmarks: la Seine, Notre Dame, Eiffel Tower (several available on the Internet)

Recap

* Où habites-tu?
* J'habite à …

Introducing the vocabulary

Discuss the types of buildings that the pupils live in.

22a Show a flashcard (made from Sheet 22a) of a house and say 'une maison'. The pupils should repeat this several times. Tell them that if you live in a house, you say, 'J'habite dans une maison.' They should repeat this phrase several times.

22a Now use the same method with 'un appartement'. If any of your pupils live in other types of dwelling, eg a houseboat (une habitation flottante) or a caravan (une caravane), introduce these words.

Activities

Children sit in a circle and they ask and answer the question around the circle. The first child says, 'Où habites-tu?' and the second child replies, giving the type of accommodation they live in, then asks 'Où habites-tu?' to the third child in the circle, and so on.

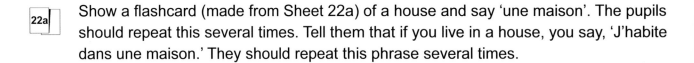 Children go around the room, asking and answering the questions learned so far.

22a If you would like to give pupils a colouring activity, they could colour in the flashcard pictures (Sheet 22a).

CD story

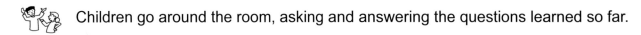 Listen to Track 8 on CD2: Marvin and Loulou go to Paris. Encourage pupils to practise the French phrases in the pauses. Show photos of the places in Paris mentioned in the story: la Seine, Notre Dame and the Eiffel Tower.

Sur le pont d'Avignon

Learning objective

✳   To sing the song 'Sur le pont d'Avignon'

Vocabulaire	Vocabulary
sur	on
le pont	the bridge
on y danse	everybody dances
tous en rond	in a circle

Resourses

✳   Sheet 23b (page 86)

✳   CD2, Track 18: Sur le pont d'Avignon (instrumental version: CD2, Track 19)

✳   Map of France

✳   Picture of the bridge at Avignon (several available on the Internet)

✳   Sheet 8a (page 36)

✳   CD2, Track 9: Marvin and Loulou visit to Avignon

Recap

✳   J'habite dans une maison/un appartement

Introducing the vocabulary/song idea

 Show a picture of the bridge at Avignon.

 Show a map of France (you could use Sheet 8a), pointing out places of interest (eg Paris, Bologne, Calais, etc) and where Avignon is situated.

Get pupils to pronounce the word, 'Avignon' correctly, repeating it several times. Then progress to 'le pont d'Avignon'.

Say, then sing the first line of the song, with pupils repeating until they can sing the line. Use CD Track 18 on CD2, if you wish.

Refrain	*Chorus*
Sur le pont d'Avignon	*On the Bridge of Avignon*
On y danse, on y danse	*Everybody dances, everybody dances,*
Sur le pont d'Avignon	*On the Bridge of Avignon*
On y danse tous en rond.	*Everybody dances in a circle.*
Les beaux messieurs font comme ça,	*The handsome gentlemen go like this,*
Et puis encore comme ça.	*And again like this.*
(Refrain)	*(Chorus)*
Les belles dames font comme ça	*The lovely ladies go like this,*
Et puis encore comme ça.	*And again like this.*
(Refrain)	*(Chorus)*

Les beaux garçons font comme ça,	*The handsome boys go like this,*
Et puis encore comme ça.	*And again like this.*
(Refrain)	*(Chorus)*
Les belles filles font comme ça	*The lovely ladies go like this,*
Et puis encore comme ça.	*And again like this.*
(Refrain)	*(Chorus)*

Introduce the remainder of the chorus in the same way.

The verses could be taught at a later date, or just stick with learning the chorus. Although pupils may find this song difficult at first, it is well worth the effort, as little ones love singing this song.

Activities

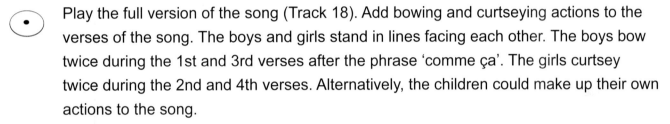

Play the full version of the song (Track 18). Add bowing and curtseying actions to the verses of the song. The boys and girls stand in lines facing each other. The boys bow twice during the 1st and 3rd verses after the phrase 'comme ça'. The girls curtsey twice during the 2nd and 4th verses. Alternatively, the children could make up their own actions to the song.

On Sheet 23a, pupils can colour in the picture and can add other features in the background.

CD story

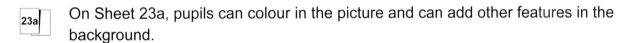

Listen to Track 9 on CD2: Marvin and Loulou visit to Avignon. Encourage pupils to practise the French phrases in the pauses.

Sur le pont d'Avignon

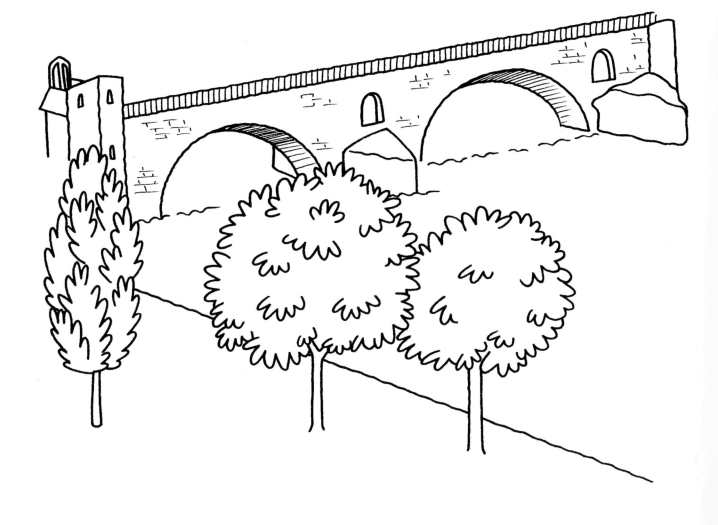

J'aime Parler!
© Ann May and Brilliant Publications

Ideas for French assemblies

You can think about doing an assembly once you have taught three songs or rhymes. Stick to three topics, or do a longer assembly at the end of the year. Introduce each topic in English. Sing songs in between role-plays. A child could translate what is being said into English.

I've found that French assemblies go down very well with parents and headteachers!

Lesson 1: Bonjour
*   Individual pupils go up to their class teacher/headteacher etc and say 'Bonjour' shaking their hand. If parents are present, pupils can say, 'Bonjour Maman/Papa' and hopefully the parent will reply.

Lessons 2 and 3: Ça va?
*   Role-play – pupils pretend they are feeling good/bad/hurt etc. Sing 'Bonjour, ça va' from *Chantez Plus Fort!*, using hand signals.

Lessons 5 and 13: C'est combien?, Les nombres 13–31
*   Chant numbers together.

*   Sing '1, 2, 3 nous irons au bois'.

Lesson 7: L'alphabet
*   Chant or sing the alphabet together, or alternate letters between two or more pupils.

*   One pupil could write down names, asking 'Comment t'appelles-tu?' and 'Comment ça s'écrit?'

Lesson 11: Les jours de la semaine
*   Say a day and a pupil mimes something they do on that day.

*   Sing or chant the days of the week rhyme.

Lesson 12: Les mois
*   Pupils chant months, standing up when it is their birthday month.

*   Sing the months rhyme.

Lessons 17 and 18: Mes frères et mes sœurs, Il/Elle s'appelle …
*   Pupils say in turn what brothers and/or sisters they have, eg 'J'ai une sœur', 'J'ai deux frères et une sœur'. If the sibling is present, they can point to him/her.

Lesson 19: Frère Jacques

∗   Sing the song while a pupil who is Frère Jacques pretends to be asleep. At the end of the song, he wakes up and rings a bell.

Lesson 23: Sur le pont d'Avignon

∗   Pupils sing and do actions to the song (girls curtsey and boys bow). This is a good song with which to finish the assembly.

Transcript of CDs

CD1, Track 1

Nar: **Marvin starts his adventure by Ann May**
Listen for the French words and phrases. Try saying the French yourself after you hear it. One day, a curious little kitten called Marvin went for a walk. He walked for a long, long way, until he came to a great big boat. He climbed onto the boat and, feeling very tired, curled up in a corner, under a seat. The boat started gently swaying from side to side, until it rocked Marvin to sleep.
Hours later, Marvin woke up, stretched and jumped off the boat. He looked around him, but he didn't know where he was. Then he heard a friendly sounding voice:

Loulou: Bonjour!
Nar: It was a beautiful French cat.
Marvin: Who are you?
Nar: Said Marvin.
Loulou: I'm Loulou. I'm French. Have you come to visit me? I see that your boat is from England. I've got lots of English friends.
Marvin: Oh! I just fell asleep. I'm Marvin. Where am I?
Loulou: You're in France now. Let me show you around.
Nar: So Loulou and Marvin went for a walk. Whenever Loulou met another cat, she would say:
Loulou: Bonjour!
Marvin: What does that mean?
Nar: Asked Marvin.
Loulou: It means 'hello'. You try to say it.
Marvin: Bonjour!
Loulou: Well done! You're speaking French now!
Nar: Monsieur and Madame Rouge and their daughter Amélie, a ginger cat family, were coming down the road. Loulou greeted Monsieur Rouge:
Loulou: Bonjour, Monsieur!
Nar: They shook paws, and Monsieur Rouge replied:
M. R: Bonjour Loulou!
Nar: Then, Loulou turned to Madame Rouge and said:
Loulou: Bonjour, Madame!
Nar: They also shook paws. Madame Rouge answered:
Mme R: Bonjour Loulou!
Nar: Then Loulou and Amélie kissed each other on both cheeks and greeted each other.
Loulou: Bonjour Mademoiselle!
Amélie: Bonjour Loulou!
Nar: The ginger cat family all looked at Marvin, who tried to copy what Loulou had said to them. To Monsieur Rouge, Marvin said:
Marvin: Bonjour Monsieur!
Nar: Monsieur Rouge answered:

M. R: Bonjour Monsieur!
Nar: To Madame Rouge, Marvin said:
Marvin: Bonjour Madame!
Nar: Madame Rouge replied:
Mme R: Bonjour Monsieur!
Nar: Marvin turned to Amélie and said:
Marvin: Bonjour Mademoiselle!
Nar: Amélie smiled at Marvin and said:
Amélie: Bonjour Monsieur!
Nar: Loulou explained that Marvin was from England and that it was his first day in France. When it was time for the ginger cat family to go home, they said:
M. R and
  Mme R: Au revoir, Loulou! Au revoir, Marvin!
Nar: To Monsieur Rouge, Marvin and Lolulou said,
Marv. &
  Loulou: Au revoir, Monsieur Rouge.
Nar: To Madame Rouge, they said,
Marv. &
  Loulou: Au revoir, Madame Rouge.
Nar: And to Amélie, they said,
Marv. &
  Loulou: Au revoir, Amélie.
Nar: Later on Marvin said to Loulou:
Marvin: I like speaking French. It's fun!
Loulou: Come on. I'll take you to my house for some food.
Nar: And off they went.
＊
See if you can remember what Marvin said in French. How did he say hello? … Bonjour!
How did he say hello to Monsieur Rouge? … Bonjour, Monsieur!
And to Madame Rouge? … Bonjour, Madame!
And to Amélie? … Bonjour, Mademoiselle!
How did he say goodbye? … Au revoir! Bravo!
And au revoir to you too!
＊＊

CD1, Track 2

Nar: **Marvin and Loulou go to the market by Ann May**
Listen for the French words and phrases. Try saying the French yourself after you hear it. Marvin, the curious little kitten, was staying with his big friend, Loulou, the French cat. He woke up one morning and found that his friend Loulou had already woken up. She smiled at Marvin and said:
Loulou: Bonjour Marvin.
Nar: Marvin replied:
Marvin: Bonjour Loulou.
Nar: Loulou was so pleased that Marvin could now speak French.

Loulou: Let me show you the market. They sell lots of things there. We might even be able to get some fish!

Nar: Marvin liked the sound of that, so off they went. At the market they saw lots of things: soap, biscuits, clothes, cheese, perfume and soon they could smell the fish!
At the soap stall, the stallholder saw Loulou and said:

SH1: Bonjour Loulou! Ça va?

Nar: Loulou replied:

Loulou: Ça va bien, merci.

Marvin: What did you say? I didn't understand.

Loulou: Ah! The stallholder asked me how I was, 'Ça va?', and I replied that I was well, 'Ça va bien, merci.'

Nar: At the biscuit stall, the stallholder saw Loulou and said:

SH2: Bonjour Loulou! Ça va?

Nar: Loulou replied:

Loulou: Ça va bien, merci.

Nar: Loulou and Marvin walked on. At the cheese stall, the stallholder saw Loulou and said:

SH3: Bonjour Loulou! Ça va?

Nar: Again, Loulou answered:

Loulou: Ça va bien, merci.

Nar: At the fish stall, the stallholder said:

SH4: Bonjour Loulou! Ça va?

Nar: This time Loulou looked a bit sad, because her tummy was rumbling, but she managed to smile weakly and said:

Loulou: Comme ci, comme ça.

Nar: Then the stallholder threw them a fish. Loulou and Marvin could not believe it. Loulou smiled and called out:

Loulou: Merci!

Marvin: Merci!

Nar: Marvin shouted as well. He had guessed that 'merci' meant 'thank you!' The stallholder asked Loulou and Marvin again:

SH4: Ça va?

Nar: This time Loulou said:

Loulou: Ça va bien, merci.

Nar: And Marvin said:

Marvin: Ça va bien, merci.

Nar: They enjoyed their fish dinner very much. Afterwards Loulou asked Marvin:

Loulou: Ça va?

Nar: And he replied:

Marvin: Ça va bien, merci!

Nar: And they started to walk home.

＊

See if you can remember the French words in this story.
What did each stallholder ask Loulou? ... Ça va?
What did Loulou reply? ... Ça va bien, merci.
What did Loulou reply at the fish stall? ... Comme ci, comme ça.
What did Loulou and Marvin say when the stallholder threw the fish? ... Merci. Très bien!
Well done, and au revoir!

＊＊

CD1, Track 3

Nar: **Marvin and Loulou visit Amélie by Ann May**
Listen for the French words and phrases. Try saying the French yourself after you hear it. Marvin and Loulou were on their way home from the market.

Loulou: I know. Let's go and see Amélie, the ginger kitten. You met her on your first day in France. Do you remember? I'm sure she'd love to play with you.

Marvin: OK.

Nar: Marvin followed Loulou to the end of the road, around a corner and over a bridge. There was Monsieur Rouge, the ginger cat, in the front garden of a big, beautiful house. Remembering his French, Marvin said to him:

Marvin: Bonjour, Monsieur. Ça va?

Nar: Monsieur Rouge frowned and said:

M. R: Ça ne va pas.

Nar: Marvin and Loulou wondered what was wrong. Monsieur Rouge turned around, beckoning them to follow him. They followed him into the house, through a long hallway and into a big white kitchen. There, in the kitchen, was Madame Rouge. Marvin said to her:

Marvin: Bonjour, Madame. Ça va?

Nar: Madame Rouge looked worried as well:

Mme R: Ça ne va pas.

Nar: Madame Rouge turned around, beckoning them to follow her. She led them to a corner of the kitchen, where there was a cat basket. In the cat basket, there was Amélie, the kitten. She was lying very still, looking at them with one eye open. Marvin said to her:

Marvin: Bonjour, Amélie. Ça va?

Amélie: Ça va mal.

Nar: Monsieur Rouge explained to Loulou that they had planned to go and visit the Eiffel Tower in Paris, but Amélie had woken up that morning with a nasty cold.

Marvin: Oh, never mind, you can go another day! I have an idea for cheering you up!

Nar: Marvin ran to the lace curtains and raced to the top as fast as he could, then hung upside down. Amélie started to laugh, because Marvin looked so funny.
All the laughing made her feel a bit better and she said:

Amélie: Ça va bien!

Nar: They all had a lovely time trying to make Amélie feel better.

＊

What did Marvin ask everybody? ... Ça va?
What did Monsieur Rouge reply? ... Ça ne va pas.
What did Madame Rouge reply? ... Ça ne va pas.
What did Amélie reply? ... Ça va mal.
What did she say when Marvin cheered her up? ... Ça va bien. Très bien!
Well done! Au revoir!

＊＊

CD1, Track 4

Nar: **Marvin and Loulou go to the playground by Ann May**

Listen for the French words and phrases. Try saying the French yourself after you hear it.

It was a lovely day, so Marvin and Loulou decided to go to the playground. Marvin had never been to a playground before and when they got there he was very excited to see the swings, the roundabout and the very long slide. Marvin and Loulou noticed a group of kittens having lots of fun. Marvin went up to the kittens and said nervously:

Marvin: Bonjour!

Nar: He was delighted when the kittens replied:

All: Bonjour!

Nar: Marvin was keen to get to know the kittens, so he asked Loulou:

Marvin: How do you ask someone their name?

Loulou: Comment t'appelles-tu?

Nar: Marvin repeated the phrase to himself:

Marvin: Comment t'appelles-tu?

Nar: When he felt ready, he went up to a little tabby kitten and asked:

Marvin: Comment t'appelles-tu?

Nar: The kitten responded:

Jac: Je m'appelle Jacques.

Marvin: Peljacques?

Nar: Wondered Marvin. Jacques smiled and corrected him:

Jac: Non. Jacques.

Marvin: Jacques?

Jac: Oui,

Nar: Said Jacques, and they went off to play together.

Nar: A bit later, a black and white kitten came up to Marvin. The kitten asked:

André: Comment t'appelles-tu?

Nar: Marvin was so pleased that he could understand!

Marvin: Je m'appelle Marvin.

Nar: Marvin then asked the kitten,

Marvin: Comment t'appelles-tu?

Nar: And the kitten replied:

André: Je m'appelle André.

Marvin: André?

André: Oui,

Nar: Said André and they went off to play on the swings together. When it was time to go, Loulou found Marvin climbing up the slide.

Loulou: It's time to go,

Nar: Loulou called. Marvin climbed to the top of the slide for one last go. He came sliding down – wheeeee! – with his eyes wide open and fur flying! Marvin called out to all his new friends:

Marvin: Au revoir!

Nar: They all replied

All: Au revoir, Marvin!

Nar: And Marvin and Loulou went off to find some tea.

✴

How did Marvin ask Jacques what his name was? … Comment t'appelles-tu?

What did Jacques reply? … Je m'appelle Jacques.

How do you say 'Yes' in French? … Oui.

How do you say 'No' in French? … Non.

How did Marvin say goodbye to his new friends? … Au revoir. Bravo!

And au revoir to you too.

✴✴

CD1, Track 5

Nar: **Marvin and Loulou go to the café by Ann May**

Listen for the French words and phrases. Try saying the French yourself after you hear it.

Loulou and Marvin were very hungry, so Loulou took Marvin to a café.

Outside the café, people were sitting at tables. Parasols were shading the people from the hot sun. The people were eating and drinking. Loulou started to walk around the peoples' legs. When she saw people that she knew, she would look up and say:

Loulou: Bonjour, ça va?

Nar: The people would reply:

Man: Bonjour Loulou! Ça va bien, et toi?

Nar: Everyone was so friendly. Loulou came to a table with no people. Marvin noticed that lots of crumbs had fallen on the ground. Loulou pointed to the crumbs and counted them.

Loulou: Un, deux, trois, quatre, cinq, six, sept, huit, neuf, dix.

Marvin: What are you doing?

Loulou: I'm counting the crumbs so that we can share them. There are 10 crumbs, so you can have 5 and I can have 5.

Nar: They soon ate up all the crumbs. Loulou found another table where everyone had gone. This time Marvin joined in the counting.

Marv. &
Loulou: Un, deux, trois, quatre, cinq, six, sept, huit, neuf, dix, onze, douze.

Nar: This time there were 12 crumbs. They shared the crumbs out and ate them up.

Then, Marvin was very naughty. He jumped up onto a table and started eating up half a tuna sandwich that had been left there. Loulou made him come down quickly, before the waitress caught him. Then off they went home.

✴

How do you count to three in French? … Un, deux, trois.

What is the French word for 'five'? … cinq.

What number comes after 'cinq, six, sept'? … huit.

How did they count the 12 crumbs? … un, deux, trois, quatre, cinq, six, sept, huit, neuf, dix, onze, douze. Excellent!

Au revoir!

✴✴

CD1, Track 6

Nar: **Marvin and Loulou visit the school by Ann May**

Listen for the French words and phrases. Try saying the French yourself after you hear it. One day, Loulou took Marvin to a place where there were lots of children. It was a school. They looked through the railings, and they could see the children playing in a playground. Marvin was curious.

Marvin: What is this place?

Loulou: It's a school.

Marvin: What's a school?

Loulou: Well, it's a place where children go to learn. They learn to read and write and learn lots of different things.

Nar: Marvin was only a little kitten, so the children seemed very big to him. Marvin and Loulou climbed through the railings and into the playground. Loulou went up to one of the children and asked:

Loulou: Quel âge as-tu?

Nar: The girl replied:

Girl: J'ai cinq ans.

Nar: Then she ran off to play with her friends. Marvin asked Loulou:

Marvin: What did you ask her?

Loulou: I asked her how old she was, 'Quel âge as-tu?'

Nar: Marvin thought he would try this out. He walked up to a boy and wrapped his tail around the boy's legs. The boy looked down at him in surprise. Marvin said to him:

Marvin: Quel âge as-tu?

Nar: The boy replied:

Boy 1: J'ai six ans.

Nar: Then he ran off to play with his friends. Marvin was delighted that the boy answered him, and even more delighted that he understood him, because he remembered that 'six' means six.

Nar: Loulou and Marvin went up to another boy. He was a little bigger. Marvin asked him,

Marvin: Quel âge as-tu?

Nar: The boy grinned and answered:

Boy 2: J'ai sept ans.

Nar: He ran off to the climbing frame.

Marvin: I understood that boy; he said he's seven!

Loulou: That's right! Well done.

Nar: Then Marvin turned to Loulou and asked her the question.

Marvin: Quel âge as-tu?

Nar: And Loulou replied:

Loulou: J'ai quatre ans.

Nar: Marvin was surprised that Loulou was four years old.

They could see lots of children were playing in a large tray. Marvin and Loulou jumped up to have a look. It was a huge sand tray. Marvin started to walk along the edge of the sand tray, but he slipped and fell in and he was covered in sand! All the children laughed at him.

Nar: Loulou reached in and pulled Marvin out of the sand. Marvin had to shake himself very hard to get all the bits of sand out of his fur. Loulou said:

Loulou: I think we'd better go home now, and get you cleaned up!

✻

How did Marvin and Loulou ask the children their age? … Quel âge as-tu?

How did the five-year-old girl reply? … J'ai cinq ans.

What did the six-year-old boy reply? … J'ai six ans.

What did Loulou reply when Marvin asked how old she was? … J'ai quatre ans. Très bien.

Au revoir!

✻✻

CD1, Track 7

Nar: **Marvin learns the alphabet by Ann May**

Nar: Listen for the French words and phrases. Try saying the French yourself after you hear it.

Nar: One day, Loulou and Marvin went to see Amélie, the little kitten who hadn't been feeling very well. When they got there, she was sitting in her basket making strange sounds:

Amélie: A, B, C, D, E, F, G, H, I, J, K, L, M, N, O, P, Q, R, S, T, U, V, W, X, Y, Z.

Marvin: Loulou, I don't think Amélie is very well yet.

Loulou: Yes she is, she's practising her alphabet!

Nar: Madame Rouge, Amélie's mother, came up to Marvin and said:

Mme R: You can learn it too, Marvin. Say these letters after me: A, B, C, D.

Marvin: A, B, C, D.

Mme R: E, F, G.

Marvin: E, F, G.

Mme R: H, I, J, K.

Marvin: H, I, J, K.

Mme R: L, M, N, O, P.

Marvin: L, M, N, O, P.

Mme R: Q, R, S.

Marvin: Q, R, S.

Mme R: T, U, V.

Marvin: T, U, V.

Mme R: W, X.

Marvin: W, X.

Mme R: Y, Z.

Marvin: Y, Z.

Nar: Marvin and Loulou spent some time practising the alphabet then, after playing with Amélie, it was time to go home.

Nar: On the way, Marvin found a biscuit on the ground, and started eating it.

Marvin: Ouch! My tooth hurts.

Loulou: Oh dear, we'd better take you to the vet.

Nar: When they got to the vet's they went inside and the receptionist said:

Rec 1: Oui, comment t'appelles-tu?

Nar: Marvin answered:

Marvin: Je m'appelle Marvin.

Nar: The receptionist asked:

Rec 1: Comment ça s'écrit?

Nar: Marvin didn't know what that meant, but Loulou understood the receptionist wanted Marvin to spell his name. She answered for him:
Loulou: M, A, R, V, I, N.
Nar: Marvin waited, and waited until the vet could see him. The vet looked inside his mouth and said:
Vet: Non.
Nar: The vet couldn't help him, so out they went. Then Loulou had another idea.
Loulou: I know, I'll take you to the doctor!
Nar: When they got to the doctor's, the receptionist said:
Rec 2: Oui, comment t'appelles-tu?
Nar: Marvin tried to smile and answered:
Marvin: Je m'appelle Marvin.
Nar: The receptionist looked up from his computer screen and asked:
Rec 2: Comment ça s'écrit?
Nar: This time Marvin understood, and he spelt out his name:
Marvin: M, A, R, V, I, N.
Nar: They waited in the waiting room, then when Marvin saw the doctor, the doctor said,
Doctor: Non.
Nar: The doctor couldn't help Marvin.
Loulou: I know what we should have done. We should have taken you to the dentist!
Nar: So off they went to the dentist's. When they got to the dentist's, the receptionist said to Marvin,
Rec 3: Oui, comment t'appelles-tu?
Nar: Marvin answered:
Marvin: Je m'appelle Marvin.
Nar: The receptionist asked:
Rec 3: Comment ça s'écrit?
Marvin: M, A, R, V, I, N.
Nar: They waited in the waiting room, and when the dentist called him in, he had a look and said,
Dentist: Oui … oui.
Nar: And he made the tooth better. When the dentist had finished, Marvin felt so happy that he jumped up onto the dentist's desk and ran around messing up all the dentist's papers! Loulou scolded:
Loulou: Ah, non! Marvin!
Nar: Marvin jumped down from the desk and Loulou took him out quickly.
Marv. &
 Loulou: Au revoir!
*
What was the first question the receptionist at the vet's asked? … Comment t'appelles-tu?
What was her other question? … Comment ça s'écrit?
How did Marvin spell his name in French? … M, A, R, V, I, N. Excellent.
Au revoir!
**

CD1, Track 8
Nar: **Marvin and Loulou go to the supermarket by Ann May**
Listen for the French words and phrases. Try saying the French yourself after you hear it. One day, Loulou and Marvin went out for a walk. Marvin said to Loulou:
Marvin: This is France, isn't it?
Loulou: Oui, la France!
Marvin: I like France.
Nar: Then they came to a supermarket. They went inside and looked at all the lovely food. They came to a cheese counter.
Loulou: Look at all the different kinds of French cheese.
Nar: Loulou pointed to a soft, creamy white cheese.
Loulou: That one is called Brie.
Marvin: Brie?
Loulou: Oui.
Nar: Marvin pointed to another cheese. It was round and white.
Marvin: What's that one called?
Loulou: Camembert.
Marvin: Camembert?
Loulou: Oui.
Nar: The man at the cheese counter noticed the two cats, and he said to them,
Man: Bonjour, ça va?
Nar: Marvin answered:
Marvin: Ça va bien merci.
Nar: The man asked:
Man: Comment t'appelles-tu?
Nar: And Marvin answered:
Marvin: Je m'appelle Marvin.
Nar: The man turned to Loulou and asked:
Man: Et comment t'appelles-tu?
Nar: Loulou responded:
Loulou: Je m'appelle Loulou.
Nar: Then they counted all the different cheeses.
Marv. &
 Loulou: Un, deux, trois, quatre, cinq, six, sept, huit, neuf, dix, onze, douze!
Nar: They had counted 12 cheeses.
Just as they were leaving the cheese counter they bumped into Madame Rouge and Amélie. There was a beautiful smell coming from Madame Rouge. Loulou said:
Loulou: Mmm, you smell nice!
Mme R: That's my perfume. It's a famous French perfume made by Chanel.
Marvin: Chanel? Mmm, that smells wonderful.
Amélie: Can you smell my perfume, Marvin? It's French too. It's made by Dior!
Marvin: Oh, Dior! I like your perfume too!
Mme R: We must continue shopping. Au revoir Loulou! Au revoir Marvin!
Nar: After Madame Rouge and Amélie had left, Marvin saw some tins piled up on top of one another. He could not resist trying to climb to the top. But when he was nearly at the top, all the tins suddenly fell down! They rolled around all over the supermarket. Loulou was horrified.

Loulou: Come on Marvin, let's go, quickly!
Nar: Loulou and Marvin ran out of the supermarket and all the way home.

*

How did Loulou say the word 'France'? … La France.
What was the name of the soft, creamy white cheese they saw? … Brie.
What was the name of the second cheese they saw? … Camembert.
Who made Madame Rouge's perfume? … Chanel.
Who made Amélie's perfume? … Dior. Bravo!
Au revoir!

**

CD1, Track 9

Nar: **Marvin and Loulou celebrate Christmas by Ann May**
Listen for the French words and phrases. Try saying the French yourself after you hear it. When Marvin looked out of the window on Christmas Eve, he had a big surprise. White flakes were falling from the sky.
Marvin: Oh, what's that?
Loulou: La neige! Snow!
Marvin: La neige?
Loulou: Oui!
Nar: Marvin was very excited as he hadn't ever been in snow before. He skidded this way and that. Loulou laughed and said:
Loulou: I have a great idea. Let's make 'des boules de neige!'
Marvin: Boules de neige? What do you mean?
Loulou: Snowballs!
Nar: Loulou said, throwing one at Marvin. Marvin repeated:
Marvin: Boules de neige.
Nar: He laughed and threw a snowball back. Playing in the snow was so much fun! They carried on walking till they came to some fields.
Loulou: See those fields? 'Les champs?'
Nar: Said Loulou, pointing to some fields covered in a white blanket of snow.
Loulou: Let's throw our snowballs in 'les champs'.
Marvin: Oui! Les champs!
Nar: Marvin threw a big ball as hard as he could into the fields. Next they came to some woods. Loulou pointed to the woods and said:
Loulou: Les bois. The woods. We could throw 'des boules de neige dans les bois!'
Marvin: Oui! Les bois!
Nar: Marvin quickly threw a snowball into the woods. They were excited by the snowy weather, but they felt so cold they decided to return home. On the way, Loulou started to sing a song:
Loulou: Vive le vent, vive le vent
Vive le vent d'hiver
Qui s'en va, sifflant, soufflant
Dans les grands sapins verts.
Oh! Vive le vent, vive le vent
Vive le vent d'hiver
Boules de neige et Jour de l'An
Et Bonne Année Grand-mère!

Nar: Marvin liked the song because it was so jolly. He recognized the bit in the song about 'boules de neige' – snowballs. When Loulou sang it again he did his best to join in with her.
Marv. &
Loulou: Vive le vent, vive le vent
Vive le vent d'hiver
Qui s'en va, sifflant, soufflant
Dans les grands sapins verts.
Oh! Vive le vent, vive le vent
Vive le vent d'hiver
Boules de neiges et Jour de l'An
Et Bonne Année Grand-mère!
Nar: When Marvin and Loulou got home they were really, really tired and fell asleep in front of the fire. The next morning Loulou woke up and she prodded Marvin on the paw, shouting:
Loulou: Joyeux Noël!
Marvin: Pardon? What are you saying?
Nar: Marvin said, rubbing his eyes.
Loulou: Joyeux Noël! Merry Christmas!
Marvin: Ah! Joyeux Noël!
Nar: Because it was Christmas day, they wanted to go and see some of their friends. Marvin practised French words as they walked along. When they went past the fields, he said:
Marvin: Les champs.
Nar: When they walked past the woods, he said:
Marvin: Les bois.
Nar: Then Marvin picked up a snowball and threw it at Loulou. He shouted:
Marvin: Des boules de neige!
Nar: Loulou quickly ducked. When they got to Amélie's house, Amélie opened the door. Loulou and Marvin said together,
Marv. &
Loulou: Joyeux Noël!
Amélie: Joyeux Noël!
Nar: Marvin and Loulou gave Amélie a little present to unwrap. It was a toy mouse. Amélie gave Marvin a little present as well. He unwrapped it, and there it was! A little toy ball to chase! Marvin was so excited, he ran out of the house, and darted around the field, covered in snow. He climbed up a tree, and down again really fast. And then off they went home, happy that it was Christmas.

*

What's the French word for snow? … la neige.
How do you say 'fields' in French? … les champs.
How do the French say 'the woods'?   les bois.
How do you say 'snowballs' in French? … boules de neige.
What did everyone say to each other on Christmas morning? … Joyeux Noël! Excellent!
Au revoir!

**

CD1, Track 10

Nar: **Amélie's New Year's Eve party by Ann May**
Listen for the French words and phrases. Try saying the French yourself after you hear it.
It was New Year's Eve. Loulou and Marvin were going to a party at Amélie's house. When they got there, they could see lots of nice food on the table. They could hear lively music playing and all the kittens were dancing! Loulou and Marvin counted the kittens:

Marv. &
Loulou: Un, deux, trois, quatre, cinq, six, sept, huit, neuf, dix, onze, douze!

Nar: Marvin went up to one of the kittens and started to talk to him,

Marvin: Comment t'appelles-tu?

Nar: The kitten replied:

Mickey: Je m'appelle Mickey.

Nar: Marvin asked the kitten:

Marvin: Quel âge as-tu?

Nar: The kitten replied:

Mickey: J'ai un an.

Nar: Marvin thought it would be polite to ask how the kitten was feeling.

Marvin: Ça va?

Nar: The kitten answered:

Mickey: Ça va bien et toi?

Marvin Ça va bien merci.

Nar: The kittens were having a great time dancing to all the music and eating all the food. And in the corner of the room was a beautiful Christmas tree. It was very, very tall and reached right up to the ceiling. There was a lot of tinsel and loads of glittery decorations on it. Marvin couldn't resist. He climbed right up to the top of the tree! Loulou saw him.

Loulou: Marvin, non!

Nar: But Marvin didn't listen. And all of a sudden, as Marvin was balancing at the top of the tree, the tree fell down, crash, on the floor! Oh dear. Marvin disappeared off into a corner. And a bit later some bells could be heard. It was midnight! And all you could hear were kittens saying:

All: Bonne Année!

Nar: Marvin didn't hear them though. He was curled up fast asleep in a corner. It was way past his bedtime.

✳

How did Marvin ask Mickey what his name was? …
    Comment t'appelles-tu?
What did Mickey reply? … Je m'appelle Mickey.
What was the next question that Marvin asked him? …
    Quel âge as-tu?
How did Mickey say his age? … J'ai un an.
What did all the kittens say when it was midnight? …
    Bonne Année! Bravo!

Au revoir!

✳✳

CD1, Track 11

Nar: **Marvin and Loulou plan an exciting week by Ann May**

Nar: Listen for the French words and phrases. Try saying the French yourself after you hear it.

Nar: Loulou and Marvin were snuggled up around the fire having a chat. They were tired after all the parties they'd been to.

Loulou: Do you like France, Marvin?

Nar: Marvin nodded enthusiastically:

Marvin: Oui!

Nar: After a short pause he asked:

Marvin: Now we've been to all these parties, what is there to look forward to?

Loulou: Well, there are lots of places to see. Lundi – we'll go to the toyshop.

Marvin: Pardon? What is 'lundi'?

Loulou: Oh, that means Monday. Lundi is the first day of the week.

Marvin: Oh, I see.

Loulou: Mardi – we'll visit Amélie,

Nar: Said Loulou. Marvin repeated:

Marvin: Mardi. Lundi, mardi.

Loulou: Mercredi – we'll visit friends at the pet shop.

Nar: Marvin practised saying all the days Loulou had said so far.

Marvin: Mercredi. Lundi, mardi, mercredi.

Loulou: Jeudi – we'll go to the farm.

Marvin: Jeudi. That must mean Thursday!

Nar: Said Marvin. He tried repeating it again:

Marvin: Jeudi

Loulou: Vendredi – we'll go to the playground.

Nar: Marvin practised saying the days again.

Marvin: Vendredi. Lundi, mardi, mercredi, jeudi, vendredi.

Loulou: Samedi – that's Saturday – we'll go to the market.

Marvin: Samedi. Lundi, mardi, mercredi, jeudi, vendredi, samedi.

Loulou: Dimanche – we'll go to the café.

Nar: Marvin repeated:

Marvin: Dimanche.

Nar: Marvin grinned:

Marvin: That must mean Sunday! I didn't know we were going to have such an exciting week. Now, let me see if I can remember all of the days of the week in French: lundi, mardi, mercredi, jeudi, vendredi, samedi, dimanche.

Nar: Marvin said the days of the week over and over again until he fell asleep.

✳

Which day of the week did Loulou start with? … lundi.
Can you remember how to say Thursday? … jeudi.
Can you remember how to say Saturday? … samedi.
Can you say all the days of the week starting with lundi? Lundi, mardi, mercredi, jeudi, vendredi, samedi, dimanche. Très bien!

Au revoir!

✳✳

CD1, Track 12

Nar: **Loulou teaches Marvin a rhyme by Ann May**
Listen for the French words and phrases. Try saying the French yourself after you hear it. Marvin was looking out of the window. It was very windy outside. He asked Loulou:

Marvin: When will the weather be nice again?

Nar: Loulou replied:

Loulou: En mars.

Marvin: Pardon?

Loulou: Mars. That means March, the third month of the year.

Marvin: What month are we now?

Loulou: Janvier – January. I know, I'll teach you the months! Listen carefully: janvier, février, mars, avril, mai, juin, juillet, août, septembre, octobre, novembre, décembre.

Nar: Then Marvin tried:

Marvin: Janvier, février… . Oh, I can't remember all of them.

Loulou: I know, I'll make up a rhyme. I'll say it one line at a time so that you can learn it.

Loulou: Janvier, février, mars, avril, mai, juin,
Juillet, août, septembre, octobre, novembre.
Décembre, Noël, vive les vacances.
Janvier, février, mars, avril, mai, juin.

Nar: Marvin listened carefully to the rhyme, so that when Loulou sang it again, he could join in:

Marv. &
Loulou: Janvier, février, mars, avril, mai, juin,
juillet, août, septembre, octobre, novembre.
Décembre, Noël, vive les vacances.
Janvier, février, mars, avril, mai, juin.

Nar: Loulou yawned.

Loulou: I'm very tired. I think I'll have a little nap.

Nar: She curled up in a ball. While she was sleeping, Marvin found a little toy ball. He chased it all around the room at top speed, but the ball got stuck under the sofa.
He lay on his side and stretched his two front paws under the sofa as far as he could, but he couldn't reach. All this reaching had made him very tired, so he left the ball under the sofa and went back to where Loulou was sleeping, and snuggled up next to her. Soon he too was fast asleep.

*

In which month did Loulou say the weather would be nice? … mars.

Which month did she say that they were in now? … janvier.

How did Marvin and Loulou say all the months? … janvier, février, mars, avril, mai, juin, juillet, août, septembre, octobre, novembre, décembre. Excellent!

Au revoir!

**

CD1, Track 13

Nar: **Marvin and Loulou go to the toyshop by Ann May**
Listen for the French words and phrases. Try saying the French yourself after you hear it. The next morning Marvin woke up early.

Marvin: What day is it Loulou?

Loulou: Lundi.

Marvin: Lundi. We must go out; we can't stay in all the time, even if the weather is cold.

Loulou: Good idea. By the way, where's my ball?

Marvin: Ah, it got stuck under that sofa, sorry.

Loulou: Never mind, it was getting very chewed. I tell you what, let's go to the toyshop then, and get another one.

Nar: So off they went to the toyshop. They went down the road and round the corner and there in front of them was the toyshop. In the window they could see all sorts of different coloured toys. They went into the shop.
In the corner of the shop was a big box of toy balls. Marvin was so excited; he reached up with his two front paws and knocked over the whole box of balls! The balls went flying and bouncing everywhere! Marvin started to count them:

Marvin: Un, deux, trois, quatre, cinq, six, sept, huit, neuf, dix, onze, douze.

Nar: Loulou carried on counting and, after a while, Marvin found that he was able to join in with her:

Loulou: Treize, quatorze, quinze, seize.
Dix-sept, dix-huit, dix-neuf, vingt.
Vingt et un, vingt-deux, vingt-trois, vingt-quatre vingt-cinq.

Marv. &
Loulou: Vingt-six, vingt-sept, vingt-huit.

Marv. &
Loulou: Vingt-neuf, trente, trente et un.

Nar: Suddenly the shop assistant came out from behind the door.

Loulou: Oh! I think we're in trouble Marvin!

Nar: Said Loulou. And they ran off.

Nar: Just as they were going out Marvin saw a toy cat. He thought it was a real cat and started to speak to it.

Marvin: Bonjour!

Nar: But there was no reply. He tried again:

Marvin: Ça va?

Nar: There was still no reply.

Marvin: Comment t'appelles-tu?

Nar: Still there was silence. Marvin decided to try one last time.

Marvin: Au revoir!

Nar: Said Marvin to the toy cat, but still it didn't reply.

Loulou: Marvin, it's just a toy cat, 'un chat'.

Nar: Marvin looked puzzled:

Marvin: Un chat?

Nar: Loulou replied,

Loulou: Yes, a cat. Oui, un chat. It won't talk to you. I think we'd better go home.

Marvin: But what about your ball?

Nar: Loulou could see the shop assistant getting closer to them.

Loulou: Um, I think we'd better go home. Come on!

Nar: So, off they scampered.

＊

How did Loulou count from 13 to 16? … treize, quatorze, quinze, seize.

How did Loulou count from 17 to 20? … dix-sept, dix-huit, dix-neuf, vingt.

How did Loulou count from 21 to 31? … vingt et un, vingt-deux, vingt-trois, vingt-quatre, vingt-cinq, vingt-six, vingt-sept, vingt-huit, vingt-neuf, trente, trente et un.

How did Loulou say 'cat' in French? … un chat.

How did Marvin say 'goodbye' to the cat? … Au revoir! Très bien.

And au revoir to you too!

＊＊

CD1, Track 14

Nar: **Marvin and Loulou go to Amélie's birthday party by Ann May**
         Listen for the French words and phrases. Try saying the French yourself after you hear it. One day Loulou and Marvin received an invitation from Amélie. It was her birthday, and she was having a party. Loulou read aloud:

Loulou: Vingt-cinq février.

Marvin: When is that?

Loulou: The 25th of February. What's the date today?

Nar: Marvin looked at the calendar.

Marvin: It's the 24th of February.

Loulou: Le vingt-quatre février. Ah, so we're going to Amélie's party tomorrow, le vingt-cinq février.

Nar: Then Loulou asked Marvin when his birthday was:

Loulou: Quelle est la date de ton anniversaire?

Nar: And Marvin replied:

Marvin: Le vingt-neuf mars.

Nar: And then Marvin asked Loulou:

Marvin: Quelle est la date de ton anniversaire, Loulou?

Nar: Loulou responded:

Loulou: Le quinze novembre.

Nar: The next day was the day of the party. Marvin and Loulou arrived at Amélie's house and met her at the door.

Marv. &
Loulou: Bon anniversaire, Amélie!

Amélie: Merci!

Nar: Marvin and Loulou gave Amélie a present. It was a toy mouse.

Amélie: Oh, merci!

Nar: Marvin went up to Monsieur Rouge and asked him when his birthday was.

Marvin: Monsieur Rouge, quelle est la date de ton anniversaire?

Nar: Monsieur Rouge replied:

M. R: Le vingt-neuf novembre.

Nar: Then Marvin went up to Madame Rouge and asked:

Marvin: Quelle est la date de ton anniversaire?

Nar: And she replied:

Mme R: Le six avril.

Nar: Suddenly the room went silent. Monsieur Rouge walked in, carrying a big cake, with candles on it. Everyone turned around to face Amélie, and they all shouted:

All: Bon anniversaire!

Nar: Then they all went to eat some party food. Marvin pushed aside the other kittens in his hurry to get to the food. One kitten fell over and cried.

Loulou: Non, Marvin. You're not allowed to push in.

Nar: Loulou led Marvin away from the food.

Marvin: Sorry,

Nar: Said Marvin, and he waited patiently for his turn to get to the birthday cake.

＊

What date was written on the party invitation? … vingt-cinq février.

How did Loulou ask Marvin when his birthday was? … Quelle est la date de ton anniversaire?

What did Marvin and Loulou say to Amélie on her birthday? … Bon anniversaire!

Now, what would you say if someone asked you, 'Quelle est la date de ton anniversaire?'

Did you say your birthday correctly? If so, très bien! Au revoir!

＊＊

CD2, Track 1

Nar: **Marvin and Loulou go to the pet shop by Ann May**
         Listen for the French words and phrases. Try saying the French yourself after you hear it. It was a nice day. Loulou and Marvin were thinking of going out. Marvin wondered what day it was.

Marvin: What day is it today, Loulou?

Loulou: Mercredi. Come and meet some other animals at the pet shop.

Marvin: Other animals? You mean not just cats?

Loulou: That's right.

Nar: Then Loulou noticed something on Marvin's whiskers.

Loulou: Qu'est-ce que c'est?

Nar: Then she realized it was some cream.

Loulou: Marvin, you're so greedy. All that cream on your whiskers!

Nar: Then Marvin said:

Marvin: What did you ask me?

Loulou: Qu'est-ce que c'est?

Marvin: What does that mean?

Nar: Marvin asked. Loulou explained:

Loulou: It means, 'What is it?'

Nar: Marvin repeated the phrase to himself.

Marvin: Qu'est-ce que c'est?

Nar: Then off they went to the pet shop. Marvin pointed to a rabbit. He said to Loulou:

Marvin: Qu'est-ce que c'est?

Nar: Loulou responded:

Loulou: C'est un lapin.

Marvin: Un lapin.

Nar:	Marvin thought he'd try talking to the rabbit:
Marvin:	Bonjour Lapin!
Nar:	The rabbit replied:
Rabbit:	Bonjour! Ça va?
Marvin:	Ça va bien merci et toi?
Nar:	The rabbit answered:
Rabbit:	Ça va bien merci.
Nar:	Then Marvin pointed to a hamster and said to Loulou:
Marvin:	Qu'est-ce que c'est?
Nar:	Loulou answered:
Loulou:	C'est un hamster.
Nar:	Marvin went up to the hamster and said:
Marvin:	Bonjour Hamster, comment t'appelles-tu?
Nar:	And the hamster replied:
Hamp:	Je m'appelle Philippe, et toi?
Marvin:	Je m'appelle Marvin.
Nar:	Then Marvin pointed to a fish, and asked:
Marvin:	Qu'est-ce que c'est, Loulou?
Nar:	Loulou answered:
Loulou:	C'est un poisson.
Nar:	The fish looked quite big to Marvin, so he wanted to know how old he was. He asked:
Marvin:	Bonjour Poisson, quel âge as tu?
Nar:	The fish replied:
Fish:	J'ai un an.
Nar:	Marvin thanked him and they walked on. Soon they came to another creature that was asleep. Marvin asked:
Marvin:	Qu'est-ce que c'est?
Loulou:	C'est un chien.
Nar:	Marvin still didn't know what the sleeping animal was. Loulou translated:
Loulou:	A dog!
Nar:	Then the dog opened one eye, saw the two cats looking at him, and he started growling and barking. Marvin was so afraid, that his fur stood on end – and he ran out of the pet shop and all the way home.

✳

How did Loulou say, 'What is this?' … Qu'est-ce que c'est?

How did Loulou say, 'It's a rabbit?' … C'est un lapin.

How did Loulou say, 'It's a hamster?' … C'est un hamster.

How did Loulou say, 'It's a fish?' C'est un poisson.

How did Loulou say 'It's a dog?' … C'est un chien. Très bien!

Au revoir!

✳✳

CD2, Track 2

Nar:	**Marvin and Loulou go for a walk by Ann May** Listen for the French words and phrases. Try saying the French yourself after you hear it. One morning, Loulou and Marvin decided to go for a walk. They were walking along the road when they heard a strange noise. It sounded like an animal of some sort. Marvin looked around and asked:
Marvin:	Qu'est-ce que c'est?

Nar:	Loulou didn't know what the animal was. So they went up to a girl who was watering some flowers in her garden. Loulou said to the girl:
Loulou:	Tu as un animal?
Nar:	The girl replied:
Girl 1:	Oui, j'ai une gerbille.
Marvin:	What did you say?
Nar:	Marvin asked. Loulou replied:
Loulou:	I asked the girl if she has a pet, and she does. She has a gerbil. But gerbils don't make that noise, so that isn't the noise we heard.
Nar:	Marvin wanted to practise saying, 'I have a gerbil':
Marvin:	J'ai une gerbille.
Nar:	They carried on walking, and they heard the funny noise again. The next house was very big, and there was a boy in the front garden. Loulou went up to the boy, and asked:
Loulou:	Tu as un animal?
Nar:	The boy nodded:
Boy 1:	Oui, j'ai un cheval!
Loulou:	He's got a horse. But it wasn't a horse making that funny noise.
Nar:	Marvin repeated:
Marvin:	J'ai un cheval.
Nar:	They kept walking along the road, and they came to another house. There was another little girl in the front garden of this house. Marvin said:
Marvin:	Shall I ask her if she's got a pet?
Loulou:	Oui.
Nar:	So Marvin went up to the little girl and said:
Marvin:	Tu as un animal?
Nar:	The girl answered:
Girl 2:	Oui, j'ai un hamster.
Marvin:	I know what that means. She's got a hamster.
Loulou:	Yes ... but a hamster doesn't make a funny noise.
Nar:	At the end of the road they came to another house, and they heard the funny noise again! It was louder this time. There was a little boy in the front garden. Marvin went up to the little boy and said to him:
Marvin:	Tu as un animal?
Nar:	And the little boy replied,
Boy 2:	Oui. J'ai un oiseau.
Nar:	Marvin asked:
Marvin:	Un oiseau?
Loulou:	Un oiseau! Yes, of course! It's a bird noise!
Nar:	The little boy brought out his bird to show Marvin and Loulou. Marvin went right up to the birdcage, and tried to stick his paw between the bars. The bird made a very loud noise. That was the noise they had been hearing ALL the time! The noise was so loud, that it made the cats run away, and they ran all the way home.

✳

What did Marvin say when he first heard the noise? … Qu'est-ce que c'est?

What did Loulou ask the first girl they met? … Tu as un animal?

How did the girl say, 'I have a gerbil?' … J'ai une gerbille.

How did the boy say, 'I have a horse?' … J'ai un cheval.

How did the second little girl say, 'I have a hamster?' … J'ai un hamster.

How did the little boy say, 'I have a bird?' … J'ai un oiseau. Très bien!

Au revoir!

✴

CD2, Track 3

Nar: **Marvin and Loulou visit a farm by Ann May**
Listen for the French words and phrases. Try saying the French yourself after you hear it. When Loulou and Marvin were out walking one day, they came to a farm. They came across a beautiful black horse. Marvin said,

Marvin: I'm going to practise my French and talk to this horse.

Nar: He went up to the horse and said:

Marvin: Bonjour, ça va?

Nar: The horse replied:

Horse: Oui, ça va bien, merci. Et toi?

Nar: Marvin answered:

Marvin: Ça va très bien, merci.

Nar: Marvin turned to Loulou:

Marvin: How do I ask the horse if he has a brother?

Loulou: Tu as un frère?

Nar: Marvin said to the horse:

Marvin: Tu as un frère?

Nar: The horse replied:

Horse: Oui, j'ai un frère.

Nar: And he pointed to a grey horse on the left side of the field. Then Marvin said to Loulou:

Marvin: How do I ask him if he has a sister?

Loulou: Tu as une sœur?

Nar: So Marvin asked the horse:

Marvin: Tu as une sœur?

Horse: Oui, j'ai une sœur.

Nar: Replied the horse and he pointed to another black horse at the back of the field. Then Marvin said to the horse:

Marvin: Au revoir!

Horse: Au revoir!

Nar: Said the horse. Marvin and Loulou carried on walking around the farm. They came to a goat. Marvin went up to the goat and said:

Marvin: Bonjour, ça va?

Goat: Ça va bien, merci.

Nar: The goat replied. Then Marvin remembered how to ask the goat if it had any brothers:

Marvin: Tu as un frère?

Nar: The goat answered:

Goat: Oui, j'ai deux frères.

Nar: She pointed to two more goats in the field. Then Marvin remembered how to ask the goat if it had any sisters:

Marvin: Tu as une sœur?

Nar: The goat pointed to two other goats nearby and said:

Goat: Oui, j'ai deux sœurs.

Marvin: Au revoir!

Nar: Marvin said to the goat, and she replied,

Goat: Au revoir!

Nar: Loulou and Marvin carried on walking around the farm, and they came to a sheep. Marvin went up to the sheep and said:

Marvin: Bonjour, ça va?

Nar: The sheep replied:

Sheep: Ça va bien, merci.

Nar: Marvin then asked the questions that he'd learnt that day:

Marvin: Tu as un frère?

Nar: The sheep replied:

Sheep: Oui, j'ai trois frères.

Nar: He pointed to three sheep on the other side of the field. Then Marvin asked:

Marvin: Tu as une sœur?

Nar: The sheep replied:

Sheep: Oui, j'ai trois sœurs.

Marvin: He pointed to another three sheep at the back of the field. Then Marvin said goodbye to the sheep:

Marvin: Au revoir!

Nar: Marvin felt so pleased with himself because all the animals had understood his French, that he felt like running around. He ran right up to a tree, and climbed up to the top of it. He tried to come down but he realized he was stuck. Loulou groaned:

Loulou: Ah, non!

Nar: She climbed up the tree, took Marvin by the paw and gently led him down the tree again. Still feeling pleased with himself, Marvin walked happily home with Loulou.

✴

How did Marvin ask the horse if he had a brother? … Tu as un frère?

How do you say, 'Yes, I have one brother?' … Oui, j'ai un frère.

How did Marvin ask the goat if she had a sister? … Tu as une sœur?

How do you say, 'Yes, I have two sisters?' … Oui, j'ai deux sœurs.

How do you say, 'I have three sisters?' … J'ai trois sœurs. Fantastique!

Au revoir!

✴✴

CD2, Track 4

Nar: **Marvin and Loulou visit the ginger cat family by Ann May**
Listen for the French words and phrases. Try saying the French yourself after you hear it. One day Loulou and Marvin decided to go and see the ginger cat family. They walked up to their house and in the front garden they found Amélie.

Marv. &
Loulou: Bonjour Amélie!

Amélie: Bonjour Loulou, Bonjour Marvin!

Nar: Then Amélie said to Loulou:

Amélie: Tu as des frères ou des sœurs?

Nar: Marvin was very happy that he understood what Amélie was asking – whether she had any brothers or sisters. Loulou replied:

Loulou: Oui, j'ai un frère, il s'appelle Patrice.

Marvin: Oh, so you've got a brother called Patrice.

Loulou: That's right,

Nar: Said Loulou. When they got to the house, they saw Monsieur Rouge inside. They called out:

Marv. &
Loulou: Bonjour Monsieur Rouge!

M. R: Bonjour Marvin, Bonjour Loulou!

Nar: Marvin thought he'd practice his French. He remembered what Amélie has just asked Loulou:

Marvin: Tu as des frères ou des sœurs?

Nar: Monsieur Rouge, who was very impressed with Marvin's French, said:

M. R: Oui, j'ai un frère, il s'appelle Thomas.

Nar: Then he added:

M. R: J'ai aussi une sœur, elle s'appelle Louise.

Nar: Marvin was so pleased he understood that Monsieur Rouge had a brother called Thomas, and a sister called Louise. Then they saw Madame Rouge. Marvin went up to her and said:

Marvin: Bonjour Madame Rouge. Tu as des frères ou des sœurs?

Nar: Madame Rouge was delighted that Marvin was so clever at speaking French. She replied:

Mme R: Oui, j'ai un frère. Il s'appelle Max.

Nar: She added:

Mme R: J'ai aussi une sœur. Elle s'appelle Natalie.

Nar: Marvin was so pleased that he understood that Madame Rouge had a brother called Max and a sister called Natalie. Then they all sat down and had a very nice tea, and they spoke lots of French together.
         After they had their tea, on the way out, Marvin saw a bright red scratching post. He sniffed all around it, and then put his two front paws on the post, got his claws out and scratched and scratched and scratched at the post. He scratched so hard, that he pulled the post right over. Marvin had to jump back quickly, so that he wouldn't get hit by it! Monsieur and Madame Rouge came running.

Mme R: Don't worry Marvin, we'll pick it up later.

Marvin: Merci et au revoir!

Nar: Said Marvin.

All: Au revoir!

Nar: And Loulou and Marvin went home.

*

How did Amélie ask Loulou if she had any brothers or sisters? … Tu as des frères ou des sœurs?

How did Monsieur Rouge say, 'Yes, I have a brother. His name is Thomas?' … Oui, j'ai un frère. Il s'appelle Thomas.

How did he say, 'I have a sister. Her name is Louise?' … J'ai une sœur. Elle s'appelle Louise.

How did Marvin say 'thank you and goodbye?' … Merci et au revoir. C'est bien!

Au revoir!

**

CD2, Track 5

Nar: Marvin and Loulou go to the beach by Ann May

         Listen for the French words and phrases. Try saying the French yourself after you hear it. One morning, Marvin looked out of the window and saw that it was a lovely, sunny day.

Marvin: Loulou, come and see what a wonderful day it is!

Loulou: Ah oui! Let's go to the beach.

Nar: Off they went, down the road, through the market square, and then they took a long stroll to the beach. When they got there, Marvin could see miles of sand stretched out before him, and the beautiful blue sea with all the boats floating on it. They found a nice spot and stretched out in the hot sun.

Nar: After a while, a family of cats came and sat nearby. One of the kittens in the family started singing a song:

Kitten: Frère Jacques, Frère Jacques
         Dormez-vous? Dormez-vous?
         Sonnez les matinées, sonnez les matinées
         Din dang dong, din dang dong.

Marvin: What's she singing about?

Loulou: Oh, it's a very famous French song. Everyone knows it. I'll teach it to you.

Nar: So Loulou taught Marvin how to sing the song, one line at a time:

Loulou: Frère Jacques, Frère Jacques

Marvin: Frère Jacques, Frère Jacques

Loulou: Dormez-vous? Dormez-vous?

Marvin: Dormez-vous? Dormez-vous?

Loulou: Sonnez les matinées, sonnez les matinées

Marvin: Sonnez les matinées, sonnez les matinées

Loulou: Din dang dong, din dang dong.

Marvin: Din dang dong, din dang dong.

Nar: The people that passed by thought that Loulou and Marvin were just meowing, but really they were singing 'Frère Jacques.'

Nar: When they had finished singing, Marvin went for a little walk around the beach. He climbed up onto a big wooden container. There was a dip in the middle of it, so Marvin snuggled into it. Then Marvin looked up and realized it was a small boat!

Nar: Suddenly a man climbed in, but he didn't see Marvin. There was a very loud noise, and then there was Marvin, with his fur standing on end, off to sea in a speedboat! Loulou gasped when she realized what had happened to Marvin.

Loulou: Oh non!

Nar: But soon enough the speedboat was back. Marvin climbed out of the boat, and Loulou was so happy that she started singing Frère Jacques all the way home.

Marv. &
Loulou: Frère Jacques, Frère Jacques …

*

How did Loulou say 'Oh yes!' in French? … Ah oui!

What sound did the bell make in the song? … Din dang
  dong.

What song did Marvin learn that day? … Frère Jacques.
  Très bien!

Why don't you try singing the song? Au revoir!

**

CD2, Track 6

Nar: **Marvin and Loulou go to see a play by Ann
  May**

  Listen for the French words and phrases. Try
  saying the French yourself after you hear it.
  One day Marvin and Loulou were invited to go
  and see a play about the Three Little Pigs. It
  was a play the mums and dads were putting
  on to entertain the children. Marvin had never
  seen a play and wondered what it was all
  about.

  That evening, they went to the theatre. They
  sat in their seats beside some other kittens,
  and looked up at the stage where there were
  some big red curtains.

  Suddenly the curtains opened – a little pig
  came onto the stage! But really, it was a cat
  in a costume. The little kitten next to Marvin
  shouted out:

Kitten 1: C'est ma mère!

Marvin: What did he say?

Loulou: He said that it's his mother.

Nar: Marvin asked the kitten:

Marvin: Comment s'appelle ta mère?

Nar: The kitten whispered back:

Kitten 1: Elle s'appelle Mimi.

Nar: Then the big bad wolf came onto the stage
  and went up to the little pig, and the same little
  kitten shouted out:

Kitten 1: C'est mon père!

Marvin: Loulou, what's he saying now?

Loulou: He's saying the wolf is his father.

Nar: Marvin whispered to the little kitten:

Marvin: Comment s'appelle ton père?

Nar: The kitten replied:

Kitten 1: Il s'appelle Paul.

Kitten 2: Chut!

Nar: A large black kitten scolded them crossly.
  Then the first little pig went off the stage and
  on came the second little pig. The kitten sitting
  behind jumped up excitedly:

Kitten 3: C'est ma mère!

Nar: Marvin turned round and asked:

Marvin: Comment s'appelle ta mère?

Nar: And the little kitten replied:

Kitten 3: Elle s'appelle Marie.

Nar: When that little pig had come off the stage, the
  third little pig came on. The little kitten behind
  them jumped up again.

Kitten 3: Oh, c'est mon père!

Nar: Marvin whispered to the little kitten.

Marvin: Comment s'appelle ton père?

Nar: The kitten replied:

Kitten 3: Il s'appelle Tim.

All: Chut!

Nar: Said all the other kittens – because you're
  really supposed to be quiet at the theatre.
  They watched the play to the end, and when
  the curtains closed the audience gave a huge
  round of applause. All the animals took a bow.
  Marvin was so excited about the play that he
  scampered right up the stage curtains and
  everyone laughed and clapped at Marvin's
  antics. And he thought to himself, 'I want to be
  in a play one day.'

*

What did the kitten next to Marvin shout when he saw
  his mother? … C'est ma mère!

What did Marvin ask the kitten? … Comment s'appelle
  ta mère?

What did the kitten shout when he saw his father?
  …C'est mon père!

What did Marvin ask the kitten this time? … Comment
  s'appelle ton père? Très bien.

Au revoir!

**

CD2, Track 7

Nar: **Marvin and Loulou go to the town square by
  Ann May**

  Listen for the French words and phrases. Try
  saying the French yourself after you hear it.
  One day, Loulou and Marvin went for a walk.

Loulou: I know, we'll go to the town square!

Nar: Marvin had never visited the town square.
  When they got there, he saw a big, paved
  square with shops and cafés all around. In the
  middle of the square there was a big fountain
  with benches near it. Marvin jumped up onto
  one of the benches where a lady was sitting.
  The lady looked at Marvin and gave him a
  stroke. Marvin liked it so much that he purred
  and purred. Then Loulou said:

Loulou: Come on Marvin, I can see some other kittens
  over there, let's go and say hello.

Nar: So they went up to the little group of kittens
  who were strolling around the town square.
  Loulou said to one of the kittens:

Loulou: Bonjour!

Nar: The kitten replied:

Kitten 1: Bonjour!

Nar: Loulou didn't know where the cat lived, so she
  asked:

Loulou: Où habites-tu?

Nar: And the kitten said:

Kitten 1: J'habite à Calais.

Nar: Then Marvin said to Loulou:

Marvin: What did you ask him?

Loulou: I asked him where he lived. I said 'Où habites-
  tu?'

Nar: Marvin repeated:

Marvin: Où habites-tu?

Marvin: I know, I'll ask someone 'Où habites-tu?'
Nar: Marvin went up to a little black kitten and said to her:
Marvin: Bonjour, comment t'appelles-tu?
Nar: The little black kitten replied:
Jessica: Je m'appelle Jessica, et toi?
Marvin: Je m'appelle Marvin.
Nar: Then Marvin tried out his new question:
Marvin: Où habites-tu?
Nar: And the little black kitten said:
Jessica: J'habite à Boulogne.
Nar: Then a tabby kitten came up to Marvin, so he said to her:
Marvin: Bonjour, comment t'appelles-tu?
Nar: The kitten answered:
Eliz: Je m'appelle Elizabeth.
Nar: Marvin asked the kitten:
Marvin: Où habites tu?
Nar: She replied:
Eliz: J'habite à Paris.
Nar: Marvin had heard of Paris because it's very famous. Elizabeth explained that she was in the town square on holiday with her friend, Antonia.
Marvin: Où habites-tu, Antonia?
Nar: Marvin asked Antonia, who was a black and white kitten, and Antonia replied:
Antonia: J'habite à Avignon.
Nar: Marvin had also heard of Avignon. Antonia said that they should come and visit her one day, and all the cats and kittens swapped addresses, so they could visit each other. By that time, they were very tired, so Marvin and Loulou went home to plan their holidays.

*

What new question did Marvin ask all the kittens? … Où habites-tu?
How do you say, 'I live in Calais?' … J'habite à Calais.
Elizabeth lives in Paris. How did she say where she lives? … J'habite à Paris.
Antonia lives in Avignon. How did she say where she lives? … J'habite à Avignon. C'est très bien!
Au revoir!
**

CD2, Track 8
Nar: **Marvin and Loulou go to Paris by Ann May**
Listen for the French words and phrases. Try saying the French yourself after you hear it. Loulou and Marvin woke up bright and early one day. It was the first day of their holiday. They were going to Paris. They walked to the train station, jumped on a train, and hid in a corner where no-one could see them. The train took them all the way to Paris. When they got to Paris, Elizabeth, the kitten, was waiting for them at the station.
Eliz: Bonjour Loulou! Bonjour Marvin!
Marv. &
Loulou: Bonjour Elizabeth!
Loulou: Ça va?
Eliz: Ça va bien merci! Let me show you Paris,

Nar: Said Elizabeth. They walked and walked, and eventually came to a very wide river.
Marvin: What's this river called?
Eliz: C'est la Seine.
Marvin: La Seine? Oh it's beautiful. And what's that church over there?
Eliz: C'est Notre Dame,
Nar: Elizabeth explained.
Eliz: It's a very famous church.
Nar: Then Marvin wondered what that dark thing was that was sticking up in the sky. It was very tall. Elizabeth explained:
Eliz: C'est la Tour Eiffel. In English you call it the Eiffel Tower.
Marvin: La Tour Eiffel.
Nar: Marvin looked at la Tour Eiffel excitedly.
Marvin: Can we go up it? Can we go to the top?
Nar: The three cats jumped into a taxi going to la Tour Eiffel. They ran past the queues of people waiting, jumped in a lift and up they went to the top of the Eiffel Tower. They could see for miles and miles, it was so beautiful.
When they came down from the Eiffel Tower, they had a walk around the little cafés and the shops in Paris. Marvin was feeling quite tired and he wanted to have a nap, so he asked Elizabeth:
Marvin: Où habites-tu?
Nar: She replied:
Eliz: J'habite dans une maison.
Nar: Elizabeth pointed to her house that they could see in the distance. On the way to the house they met some of Elizabeth's friends. When they had all said hello and asked how they were, Loulou asked one of them where he lived.
Loulou: Où habites-tu?
Nar: The kitten pointed to a block of flats and said:
Kitten 1: J'habite dans un appartement.
Nar: And then Loulou asked another kitten:
Loulou: Où habites-tu?
Nar: The kitten pointed to the same block of flats and said:
Kitten 2: J'habite dans un appartement.
Nar: There was one other friend of Elizabeth's, a big black furry kitten, and Marvin said to him:
Marvin: Où habites-tu?
Nar: The kitten pointed to a house very near them and said:
Kitten 3: J'habite dans une maison.
Nar: The friends left and everyone said 'au revoir'.
Marvin: I like your friends, Elizabeth,
Nar: Said Marvin, yawning.
Eliz: Come on. Come into my house. We'll have some tea and then we'll curl up and have a nice sleep.
Nar: And that is just what they did.
*
What was the name of the river they saw? … La Seine.
What was the name of the big church? … Notre Dame.

How do you say, 'the Eiffel Tower' in French? ... La Tour Eiffel.

How did Marvin ask Elizabeth where she lived? ... Où habites-tu?

What did she reply?... J'habite dans une maison.

How do you say 'I live in a flat?' ... J'habite dans un appartement. Excellent!

Au revoir!

✳✳

CD2, Track 9

Nar: **Marvin and Loulou visit Avignon by Ann May**

Listen for the French words and phrases. Try saying the French yourself after you hear it. Loulou and Marvin were on their way to visit Antonia in Avignon. They jumped on a train and found a corner to curl up in. It was quite a long journey so they had a nice little sleep.

Then, they woke up with a start. There they were – Avignon station! They jumped off the train and, there on the platform, they saw Antonia waiting for them. She called out:

Antonia: Bonjour Marvin! Bonjour Loulou!

Nar: They both replied:

Marv. &
 Loulou: Bonjour Antonia!

Nar: They were all so pleased to see each other again. When they finished saying 'bonjour', they followed her out of the station and into the street. Marvin asked:

Marvin: Où habites-tu?

Nar: Antonia answered:

Antonia: J'habite dans une maison.

Nar: She pointed towards a long road. On the way to Antonia's house they saw a beautiful, old bridge that had partly fallen down. It was the bridge of Avignon. Loulou felt like singing a song again. She sang slowly so that Marvin could join in:

Loulou: Sur le pont d'Avignon
On y danse, on y danse
Sur le pont d'Avignon
On y danse tous en rond.

Marv. &
 Loulou: Sur le pont d'Avignon
On y danse, on y danse
Sur le pont d'Avignon
On y danse tous en rond.

Nar: Then off they went for their new adventure in Avignon with Antonia. It was such a lovely place that they decided to stay there for the whole of the summer.

Nar: When they got to Antonia's house, Antonia showed them to their room, Marvin said to Loulou:

Marvin: Thank you for being my friend. I want to stay in France with you forever.

Nar: Marvin and Loulou snuggled up and had a nice sleep after their long journey.

✳

How did Marvin ask Antonia where she lived? ... Où habites-tu?

What did she reply? ... J'habite dans une maison.

What song did they sing when they got to the bridge? Sur le pont d'Avignon ... C'est fantastique!

Why don't you have a go singing the song? Au revoir!

✳✳

CD2, Track 10
1,2 3 nous irons au bois (sung)

✳

CD2, Track 11
1, 2, 3 nous irons au bois (instrumental)

✳

CD2, Track 12
Vive le vent (sung)

✳

CD2, Track 13
Vive le vent (instrumental)

✳

CD2, Track 14
Les mois de l'an (sung)

✳

CD2, Track 15
Les mois de l'an (instrumental)

✳

CD2, Track 16
Frère Jacques (sung)

✳

CD2, Track 17
Frère Jacques (instrumental)

✳

CD2, Track 18
Sur le pont d'Avignon (sung)

✳

CD2, Track 19
Sur le pont d'Avignon (instrumental)

✳✳

Useful resources

Brilliant Publications
BEBC Distribution, Albion Close, Parkstone, Poole BH12 3LL
www.brilliantpublications.co.uk

www.amazon.fr

Grant & Cutler Ltd
55–57 Great Marlborough Street, London W1F 7AF
www.grantandcutler.com

Language Stickers Company Ltd
Station Road, Arlesey, Bedfordshire SG15 6RG
www.languagestickers.co.uk

Last Word Resources
PO Box 1048, Stoke-on-Trent ST7 2FD
www.lastwordresources.co.uk

Little Linguists
PO Box 135, Plymouth PL4 8WZ
www.little-linguist.co.uk

Wildgoose Educational Resources
Bluesky International Ltd, The Old Toy Factory, Jackson Street, Coalville, Leicestershire
LE67 3NR
www.wildgoose.ac